Nora Hughes

The Mother of All Magic
Egyptian Rituals for Protection and Healing

Original Title: A Mãe das as Magias
Copyright © 2025, publicado por Luiz Antonio dos Santos ME.

Este livro é uma obra de não-ficção que explora os rituais egípcios voltados para proteção e cura. Através de uma abordagem abrangente, a autora apresenta práticas ancestrais utilizadas pelos sacerdotes do Antigo Egito para equilibrar energias, afastar influências negativas e promover a harmonia espiritual e física.

1ª Edição

Equipe de Produção
Autor: Nora Hughes
Editor: Luiz Santos
Capa: Studios Booklas
Diagramação: Rafael Mello
Tradução: Helena Costa
Professor Consultor: Dr. Marcelo Fontes
Pesquisadores: Ana Beatriz Lima, Caio Monteiro, Sofia Martins

Publicação e Identificação
The Mother of All Magic
Booklas, 2025
Categorias: Espiritualidade/ História das Religiões
DDC: 299.31 – CDU: 133.43

Todos os direitos reservados a:
Luiz Antonio dos Santos ME / Booklas

Nenhuma parte deste livro pode ser reproduzida, armazenada num sistema de recuperação ou transmitida por qualquer meio — eletrônico, mecânico, fotocópia, gravação ou outro — sem a autorização prévia e expressa do detentor dos direitos autorais.

Sumário

Sistemátic Index 5
Prologue 11
Chapter 1 Mystical Rituals 15
Chapter 2 Rituals of Healing and Physical Renewal 22
Chapter 3 Rituals of Prosperity and Abundance 30
Chapter 4 Rituals of Connection with the Gods 38
Chapter 5 Rituals for Victory in Battles and Conflicts 45
Chapter 6 Rituals of Protection and Spiritual Defense 53
Chapter 7 Rituals of Life Renewal 62
Chapter 8 Rituals of Love and Union 70
Chapter 9 Rituals of Justice and Balance 78
Chapter 10 Rituals of Wisdom and Knowledge 87
Chapter 11 Rituals of Purification and Spiritual Cleansing 96
Chapter 12 Protection Rituals against Curses and Evil Spirits . 106
Chapter 13 Rituals for Good Luck and Fortune 113
Chapter 14 Rituals of Rebirth and Transformation 119
Chapter 15 Rituals of Conquest and Territorial Expansion 123
Chapter 16 Rituals of Communication with Ancestors 128
Chapter 17 Rituals of Negative Energy Transformation 133
Chapter 18 Rituals of Fertility and Agricultural Growth 138
Chapter 19 Rituals of Peace and Harmony 144
Chapter 20 Rituals for the Protection of Children and Families 151
Chapter 21 Rituals of Social and Political Transformation 158
Chapter 22 Preparation Rituals for the Afterlife 164
Chapter 23 Death Rituals and the Passage to the Afterlife 171

Chapter 24 Post-Mortem Protection Rituals 179
Chapter 25 Rituals of Connection with the Cosmos and the Stars
.... 185
Chapter 26 Rituals of Spiritual Ascension and Union with the
Gods 190
Epilogue 194

Sistemátic Index

Chapter 1: Mystical Rituals - This chapter delves into the mystical heart of ancient Egyptian spirituality, exploring the concept of *ma'at* (cosmic harmony) and the Egyptians' intricate relationship with the divine and the forces governing the universe.

Chapter 2: Rituals of Healing and Physical Renewal - This chapter explores the ancient Egyptian perspective on health and healing, examining the connection between spiritual balance and physical well-being, and the role of rituals in restoring harmony to the body and soul.

Chapter 3: Rituals of Prosperity and Abundance - This chapter delves into the ancient Egyptian concept of prosperity, its connection to divine benevolence and the rituals performed to ensure the fertility of the land, abundance in harvests, and individual success.

Chapter 4: Rituals of Connection with the Gods - This chapter explores the ancient Egyptian belief in spiritual ascension and the rituals performed to achieve union with the divine, including purification practices, meditation, offerings, and the incorporation of the gods.

Chapter 5: Rituals for Victory in Battles and Conflicts - This chapter examines the ancient Egyptian belief in the divine influence on battles and the rituals performed to ensure victory, including the invocation of warrior gods, weapon consecration, and the spiritual protection of warriors.

Chapter 6: Rituals of Protection and Spiritual Defense - This chapter explores the ancient Egyptian concept of spiritual protection, the rituals performed to ward off negative energies and entities, and the use of amulets, incantations, and the invocation of guardian deities.

Chapter 7: Rituals of Life Renewal - This chapter delves into the ancient Egyptian understanding of fertility as a sacred force, the rituals performed to ensure the continuity of life, and the invocation of goddesses like Isis and Hathor to bless human and agricultural fertility.

Chapter 8: Rituals of Love and Union - This chapter explores the ancient Egyptian perspective on love as a sacred force, the rituals performed to bless marital unions, and the role of deities like Hathor and Isis in ensuring harmony and reconciliation in relationships.

Chapter 9: Rituals of Justice and Balance - This chapter examines the central concept of Ma'at in ancient Egyptian spirituality, the rituals performed to maintain cosmic order, truth, and justice, and the importance of living in accordance with Ma'at for a balanced life and favorable judgment in the afterlife.

Chapter 10: Rituals of Wisdom and Knowledge - This chapter explores the ancient Egyptian quest for wisdom as a spiritual journey, the rituals performed to connect with Thoth, the god of writing and wisdom, and the role of scribes, priests, and sacred texts in acquiring and preserving knowledge.

Chapter 11: Rituals of Purification and Spiritual Cleansing - This chapter delves into the ancient Egyptian emphasis on purity and renewal, the rituals performed to cleanse the body and spirit, and the use of water, incense, amulets, and collective ceremonies to restore spiritual balance.

Chapter 12: Protection Rituals against Curses and Evil Spirits - This chapter examines the ancient Egyptian belief in negative energies and evil spirits, the rituals performed to ward off curses and protect individuals and communities, and the use of amulets, incantations, and magic circles for spiritual defense.

Chapter 13: Rituals for Good Luck and Fortune - This chapter explores the ancient Egyptian concept of luck and fortune, the rituals performed to attract prosperity and divine blessings, the role of deities like Hapi and Hathor, and the use of amulets, offerings, and enchantments to ensure good fortune.

Chapter 14: Rituals of Rebirth and Transformation - This chapter delves into the ancient Egyptian belief in rebirth and the transformative power of death, exploring the myth of Osiris and the rituals performed to prepare individuals for the spiritual journey through the underworld and achieve eternal life.

Chapter 15: Rituals of Conquest and Territorial Expansion - This chapter examines the ancient Egyptian approach to territorial expansion as a divine mission, the rituals performed to ensure victory in battle, and the role of gods like Montu and Amun-Ra in protecting and guiding the pharaoh and his army.

Chapter 16: Rituals of Communication with Ancestors - This chapter explores the ancient Egyptian belief in the continued presence of ancestors, the rituals performed to honor and communicate with them, and the role of oracles and priests in interpreting messages from the spiritual realm.

Chapter 17: Rituals of Negative Energy Transformation - This chapter delves into the ancient Egyptian understanding of energy as a malleable force, the rituals performed to transform negative energies into positive ones, and the role of Thoth, Bastet, and other deities in restoring spiritual balance.

Chapter 18: Rituals of Fertility and Agricultural Growth - This chapter examines the ancient Egyptian connection between agriculture and the divine, the rituals performed to ensure fertility and abundant harvests, and the role of gods like Min and Hapi in blessing the land and crops.

Chapter 19: Rituals of Peace and Harmony - This chapter explores the ancient Egyptian concept of Ma'at as the foundation for peace and harmony, the rituals performed to maintain balance within the kingdom and between nations, and the role of the pharaoh, priests, and community in ensuring social and political stability.

Chapter 20: Rituals for the Protection of Children and Families - This chapter delves into the ancient Egyptian emphasis on family protection, the rituals performed to ensure the safety and well-being of children and homes, and the role of deities like Hathor, Bes, and Bastet in warding off evil and maintaining harmony within the family unit.

Chapter 21: Rituals of Social and Political Transformation - This chapter examines the ancient Egyptian coronation ceremony as a cosmic event, the pharaoh's role as a divine intermediary, and the rituals performed to ensure the continuity of power, social harmony, and the preservation of Ma'at within the kingdom.

Chapter 22: Preparation Rituals for the Afterlife - This chapter explores the ancient Egyptian belief in the afterlife and the meticulous preparations made for the journey through the underworld, including tomb construction, embalming, funerary rituals, and the use of sacred texts and amulets to ensure a safe passage.

Chapter 23: Death Rituals and the Passage to the Afterlife - This chapter delves into the ancient Egyptian death rituals, including purification, embalming, the use of funerary masks, sacred texts, and amulets, and the journey of the soul through the Duat, culminating in the judgment before Osiris.

Chapter 24: Post-Mortem Protection Rituals - This chapter examines the ancient Egyptian rituals performed after death to ensure the continued protection of the soul, including offerings, prayers, the role of priests in preserving the deceased's memory, and the use of amulets and enchantments to guide the soul through the afterlife.

Chapter 25: Rituals of Connection with the Cosmos and the Stars - This chapter explores the ancient Egyptian connection to the cosmos, the alignment of temples with astronomical events, the observation of stars and planets, and the rituals performed to maintain balance between cosmic cycles and life on Earth.

Chapter 26: Rituals of Spiritual Ascension and Union with the Gods - This chapter delves into the ancient Egyptian belief in spiritual ascension, the rituals performed by the pharaoh to achieve union with the gods, and the transformative journey of purification, meditation, and invocation that connected the pharaoh to the divine realm.

Prologue

The ancient Egyptians possessed a profound knowledge of the universe and its invisible forces, something that has been lost over the millennia. Unlike any other culture, they are mentioned in the Bible itself as the only ones capable of practicing true magic. The pharaoh's magicians, in the confrontation with Moses, demonstrated that they mastered mystical abilities that went beyond the ordinary, proving that their connection to the divine and the occult transcended the limits of what we know today. In that episode, Egyptian magic was not a trick of illusion, but a tangible manifestation of the energies that permeate the cosmos.

What has been forgotten by modern humanity is that these forces, which were once so vivid and palpable, continue to exist. However, with the advancement of rationality and skepticism, we have distanced ourselves from ancient wisdom. The contemporary world, obsessed with technology and science, has relegated these practices to myths and legends. However, the truth remains: the Egyptians, more than any other people, were deeply connected to the gods and the forces that govern the balance of the universe. Their magic was a direct reflection of this intimate and powerful relationship with the divine.

The temples erected on the banks of the Nile were much more than mere religious buildings; they were portals to another reality. There, the priests invoked gods and hidden energies to shape physical reality, protecting and healing their fellow men. Amulets, such as the Eye of Horus and the scarab, contained powers that went beyond the symbolic. These small pieces were charged with the energy of the gods, and their effectiveness was proven in rituals of healing, prosperity and protection.

Time, however, has been cruel. Modernity has distanced humanity from this power. Our mechanistic view of the world has made us forget that, behind the veil of matter, there is a more complex and subtle structure. The ancients knew this. They understood that every word, every gesture and every symbol had a specific purpose, acting as channels to manipulate the invisible. The practice of magic, especially among the Egyptians, was not a primitive superstition, but a sophisticated way to interact with cosmic forces.

In a world that seems increasingly distant from the spiritual, this book offers a bridge to recover this lost knowledge. Here, you will discover not only the ritual practices that the Egyptian priests performed to maintain the balance between chaos and order, but also how these practices can be applied in the present, rescuing the latent power that still pulsates in the universe.

The rituals described in this book are not merely a historical re-reading. They are practical guides that, when applied with the proper intention, can reactivate the connection that humanity once had with the gods and with the hidden forces. You will learn how to protect yourself from negative influences, how to bring balance to your life and even how to attract prosperity, using the same principles that the Egyptians mastered. Each ritual, each symbol charged with power, opens like a key to hidden reality.

In ancient times, the Egyptians understood that the visible and the invisible are two sides of the same coin. They recognized the importance of ma'at - the cosmic balance - and dedicated their lives to maintaining this harmony, both for the kingdom and for their personal lives. Today, chaos often dominates the modern world, whether through stress, economic crises or personal challenges. But just as the Egyptians used their magic to restore order, you too can access these ancient tools to bring harmony to your daily life.

The knowledge offered here is not just a window to the past, but a revelation that still echoes with relevance today. Each chapter reveals secrets that have long been hidden, just waiting for the right seeker to bring them back to light. The Egyptians, with their reverence for divine forces and their unparalleled ability to connect to them, left a legacy of power, a legacy that can still be accessed.

Reading this book is not a simple act of absorbing information. It is an invitation to dive into a world of possibilities, where the spiritual and the material meet. It is a journey that promises not only knowledge, but transformation. You will discover that the forces that the ancients invoked are still present, waiting for those who are ready to claim the power that is rightfully theirs.

The past and the present are not disconnected; they meet here. The practices that the Egyptians mastered have not been forgotten, only dormant. Now, by opening the pages of this book, you will be called to awaken them. By understanding and applying the teachings revealed here, you will not only be exploring the mystery of ancient Egypt, but also rediscovering what humanity, in its race for progress, has left behind.

Prepare yourself, for magic, the true and profound magic that transcends time, still lives. The ancient gods are still here, watching, waiting. All you need to do is take the first step and allow yourself to reconnect with these primordial forces. By the end of this reading, you will not be the same. The power, wisdom and connection that the Egyptians cultivated for millennia can, once again, be part of your reality.

Chapter 1
Mystical Rituals

Ancient Egypt, with its fertile banks along the Nile, emerged as a civilization deeply connected to the spiritual and mystical forces that they believed governed the universe. For the Egyptians, the world was not just a physical reality, but a stage where invisible energies and powerful gods orchestrated life and death. The belief in cosmic harmony, ma'at, was the foundation upon which their culture and spirituality were built. Ma'at represented the universal order, a balance that permeated everything, from the stars to the simplest human acts. This sacred concept dictated that everyone, from the pharaoh to the peasants, had a duty to maintain the harmony of the cosmos through rituals and correct behavior.

Rituals, then, were not mere formalities. They were bridges between the visible and invisible world, a necessary link to ensure that divine order prevailed over chaos. Chaos, known as isfet, was always lurking, ready to devour harmony if humans failed in their spiritual obligations. Thus, the Egyptians sought in their rituals a way to maintain the balance between light and darkness, good and evil, life and death.

Among the gods that formed the Egyptian pantheon, each played a fundamental role in this balance. The Egyptian religion was polytheistic, with gods and goddesses who not only ruled the forces of nature, but also represented internal aspects of human life. Isis, goddess of magic and motherhood, and Osiris, god of the afterlife, occupied central places in Egyptian myths, while Ra, the sun god, traveled daily across the sky, waging his battle against the serpent Apep to ensure the return of light. These stories were not seen as mere allegories, but as parallel realities, in which the gods incessantly performed their duties so that the cosmos could continue to exist.

Within this intricate spiritual universe, priests and priestesses played a role of paramount importance. Considered mediators between the divine and the human, they held the knowledge of rituals, sacred texts and magic necessary to lead the people and the pharaoh himself to an existence in accordance with ma'at. It was they who performed the daily ceremonies in the temples, feeding the statues of the gods with offerings to ensure their good disposition. The priests were more than religious figures; they were counselors, healers and, often, the intermediaries in times of crisis.

The pharaoh himself was seen as a living god, an incarnation of Horus on earth, and, after his death, he became a manifestation of Osiris, the lord of the underworld. Ruling Egypt was not just a political function, but a sacred duty, in which the pharaoh acted as guardian of ma'at. Any imbalance in nature, such as a drought or a catastrophic flood, was seen as a failure of the sovereign to fulfill his spiritual role.

Egyptian rituals were not limited to solemn and grandiose events. They permeated all aspects of daily life, from birth to death. Smaller but equally important ceremonies took place in homes and villages, where families invoked the protection of the gods to ensure health, prosperity and safety. Amulets, prayers and small offerings were part of ordinary life, connecting each individual to this vast spiritual system.

In each of these rituals, the presence of the gods was invoked through symbols, gestures and words that contained a profound power. Words, for the Egyptians, possessed an almost magical force. When pronounced by trained priests, they could influence the course of events and transform reality. It was believed that the hymns and incantations recited during the rituals had the ability to invoke the real presence of the deities, whether to bless the pharaoh in his military campaigns or to ensure the fertility of the land.

Faced with this spiritual perspective, death was not seen as the end, but as a transition to another state of existence. The Egyptians firmly believed in the afterlife, where the soul, after facing the judgments of the underworld, could live eternally in the field of reeds, a paradise where ma'at was preserved in its purest form. But to reach this destination, the individual needed to be purified and prepared through specific rituals, from the embalming process to the daily offerings made in the tombs.

This holistic view of life and death permeated every aspect of Egyptian civilization. Every gesture, every word, every ceremony had a greater spiritual purpose, contributing to the universal balance.

Upon entering the temples of ancient Egypt, it was like stepping through a portal between two worlds. These monumental constructions, erected with a precision that sought to align the terrestrial with the celestial, were much more than mere places of worship; they represented the dwelling place of the gods on Earth. The stone that supported the temples, polished by time and adorned with sacred hieroglyphs, guarded the essence of a civilization that believed in the vital force of rituals to maintain cosmic balance. In each column, in each room darkened by incense, the presence of the divine was tangible.

The temples, distributed along the Nile, functioned as the epicenter of religious practices. Each of them, consecrated to a particular deity, was designed to reflect the celestial abode of the god to whom it was dedicated. It was believed that, within their interiors, the gods inhabited sacred statues that received daily offerings. For the Egyptians, the ritual of feeding and caring for these statues was not merely symbolic; it was a necessity to ensure that the deities maintained their benevolence and protection over the people. The pharaoh, as divine mediator, was the first priest of all temples, but, in practice, it was up to the priests and priestesses to perform the complex daily rites.

Every aspect of these rituals within the temple followed a strict order. The cleaning and purification of the sacred spaces were carried out meticulously, preparing the environment for interaction with the divine. The use of aromatic incense and the smoke that slowly rose to the heavens symbolized the prayers of mortals reaching the gods. At the heart of these rituals was the offering. Food, flowers, perfumes and precious objects were carefully arranged before the statues, in acts that symbolized human gratitude for the abundance received from the heavens.

Offerings, however, were not limited to the purpose of pleasing the gods; there was in them an intention to reestablish ma'at. The relationships between men and the gods were built on the premise of reciprocity. The gods protected, gave abundant harvests and guaranteed prosperity, but, in return, they expected to be revered and nurtured. The annual ceremonies and festivals, such as those dedicated to Ra or Isis, were crucial moments of renewal of this sacred alliance, where the temples overflowed with offerings in celebrations that united the cycle of nature with the sacred.

One of the most striking rituals performed in the temples was that of food offerings, a profound gesture of spiritual connection. The food offered to the gods, through the statues, was prepared according to ancient traditions, and after the offering, the food was often redistributed among the priests and faithful, in a continuous cycle of communion. What the gods did not consume spiritually was given back to the people, carrying a sacred energy that brought blessings and protection.

Another essential element in the rituals was the use of sacred texts, inscribed on papyri and walls. These scriptures were much more than religious records; they were formulas of spiritual power. Reciting them in the correct context could influence supernatural forces in favor of those who pronounced them. The priests mastered these texts and chanted them with almost magical precision, their voices echoing in the dark chambers of the temples, reinforcing the power of words in reestablishing ma'at.

The temples were also places of healing and transformation. In addition to their ritualistic function, many temples functioned as centers of wisdom, where the secrets of medicine and magic were studied and applied. In times of crisis, the temples became refuges where the needy sought divine intervention through the priests. Medicinal plants, amulets, incantations and prayers were used in specific rituals for the healing of diseases, reinforcing the belief that all disease had a spiritual, and not just physical, origin.

Religious festivals were times when the doors of the temples were opened to the people, breaking the barrier between the everyday and the sacred. During these events, the statues of the gods were carried in processions, moving through the streets, being acclaimed and venerated. It was a spectacle of color, light and music, where everyone participated, from the nobles to the humblest. The processions were laden with deep meanings, symbolizing the continuous movement of the gods over the world and their role as spiritual guides for humanity.

Each ceremony performed inside or outside the temples had a clear and directed purpose, an intention to shape reality through ritualistic practice. It was not just about following traditions, but about living in communion with the forces that governed the cosmos, understanding that humans were part of an eternal cycle that began with the gods and ended with themselves.

The temples, with their imposing facades and deep mysteries, continue to fascinate us. They were not just buildings, but portals that connected man to the divine, the visible to the invisible. And, above all, they were places where ma'at could be restored, a continuous and sacred task, so that the cosmic order would never be interrupted.

Chapter 2
Rituals of Healing and Physical Renewal

For the ancient Egyptians, health was not simply a physical matter. It was deeply rooted in spiritual balance and the harmony of the body with the cosmos. They believed that all illnesses arose from an imbalance in ma'at, the principle of order and justice that governed the universe. When this balance was disturbed, chaos, or isfet, manifested in the form of diseases and illnesses. Thus, healing rituals did not only treat physical symptoms but sought to restore the spiritual alignment that allowed the body to recover its natural harmony.

The gods played a central role in this process. Sekhmet, the goddess of war and healing, represented both destruction and renewal. Although she was associated with fury and disease, she was also invoked to ward off these same negative forces. It was believed that her presence could purify the body and rid the sick of their ailments. Isis, in turn, was revered as the great healer, known for her powers of magic and transformation, often called upon to protect and restore the health of children and adults.

Amulets played a vital role in healing rituals. The Egyptians believed that these objects possessed powerful energies capable of repelling diseases and bad influences. One of the most common was the Udjat, the Eye of Horus, which represented protection and restorative power. It was common for the sick to wear these amulets or place them in their homes to ward off evil forces that could aggravate their conditions. Other symbols, such as the scarab, were also used, as it was believed that these amulets had the power to regenerate life.

Healing rituals also involved the use of medicinal plants, carefully selected by priests and priest-doctors. Knowledge about the properties of plants was considered a divine gift, transmitted to humans by the gods. Garlic, onion, and myrrh were just some of the substances used, and each had a specific role in purifying the body or fighting infections. These ingredients, mixed with incense and aromatic resins, were often used in ointments or burned as offerings, filling the air with their healing aromas.

Water, especially the sacred water of the Nile, played a fundamental role in healing rituals. The Nile was seen as a source of life and rebirth, and its waters were considered a direct channel of spiritual purification. During rituals, water was used to bathe the sick person's body, purifying it both physically and spiritually. Whether in large ceremonies in temples or in simpler domestic rites, water was always an essential element of healing.

Another powerful component of these rituals was the word. The belief in the power of words and incantations was profound in Egyptian culture. Words were not just sounds; they carried their own energy, capable of influencing the spiritual and physical world. The incantations were carefully pronounced by the priests, who had the proper training to ensure that each word had the desired effect. Prayers were addressed directly to the gods, asking for their direct intervention to restore balance and expel the evil forces responsible for the illness.

In temples, the healing ritual often began with the purification of the patient. The sick person was led to a sacred environment, where the forces of chaos could not penetrate. There, bathed in sacred waters and enveloped by the aroma of purifying incense, they were placed before the statues of the gods, with offerings of food and flowers. The priest would then recite incantations and invocations for the power of the gods to flow into the patient's body, restoring their health and expelling the disease. Often, amulets were placed on the body, and the sick person received a talisman that they should carry with them to continue to be protected.

The invocation techniques varied according to the nature of the disease. For physical illnesses, rituals involving purification and baths were common. For ailments believed to be caused by spirits or evil forces, the rites could involve more complex offerings, such as sacrifices of small animals or specific foods, accompanied by more intense incantations. The presence of a priest-doctor was fundamental, as he not only understood the healing properties of natural elements but also had knowledge of the spiritual forces that needed to be manipulated.

These priest-doctors were unique figures, uniting knowledge of medicine and spirituality. They mastered both the science of herbs and physical healing as well as the knowledge of sacred texts and incantations. In many cases, they were responsible for diagnosing the spiritual origin of a disease, even before treating its physical symptoms. The imbalance of the ka, the vital force of an individual, was one of the main causes of illness, and the priest-doctor, with his knowledge of energies and magic, knew how to restore this balance through rituals, prayers, and remedies.

Thus, the healing process in ancient Egypt was a complete journey, involving both body and spirit. The rituals had the power to restore not only physical health but also spiritual well-being, allowing the individual to return to their natural state of harmony with the cosmos. For the Egyptians, healing was a way of restoring ma'at within the body, and each ritual performed was a small act of reconstruction of the universal order.

Healing in ancient Egypt was a spiritual science, where the power of the gods and the forces of nature intertwined to restore health and balance to bodies. Amidst the deepest healing rituals, the role of priest-doctors emerged prominently. These highly respected individuals not only possessed knowledge of the functioning of the human body but also understood the mysteries that connected physical health to the spiritual world. It was believed that they were able to unravel the hidden causes of a disease, going beyond the visible symptoms, to identify the spiritual forces or imbalances that needed to be corrected.

The practice of medicine in ancient Egypt was directly connected to magic, and this was evident in the complex ways in which healing was approached. There was no clear distinction between medical science and sacred rituals, as both operated under the same understanding: that the body and spirit were inseparable. Each disease was a manifestation of a spiritual imbalance, and each cure involved appealing to both the divinities and natural resources.

The priest-doctors, known as "sunu", were experts in using magic formulas and specific incantations for each illness. They possessed vast knowledge of sacred texts, which detailed healing formulas passed down by the gods. Each formula carried a magical essence, and its recitation in healing rituals was fundamental. The words spoken during treatment were not just sounds; they were invocations of power that, when uttered correctly, had the potential to alter the physical and spiritual reality of the sick person.

A notable example of this practice was the use of the so-called "Books of Medical Magic". These sacred texts, many of which were kept in temples or in private collections of priests, contained detailed incantations that were to be recited during the healing process. The magic formulas not only invoked the intervention of the gods but also contained precise instructions on the remedies that should be used in conjunction with the sacred words. Sacred water, scented oils, and medicinal herbs were often applied to the patient's body while the incantations were recited, reinforcing the belief that both - the physical and the spiritual - were interconnected.

Among the most common rituals, the use of sacred water was one of the most symbolic and powerful. The water of the Nile, considered the very essence of life, was often used in rituals of purification and healing. It was common for the sick to be bathed with sacred water, in an attempt to wash away the impurities and chaos that disturbed the body. This process symbolized rebirth, where the patient, purified of negative influences, could be reborn in harmony with ma'at. It was believed that water possessed healing properties, amplified by the prayers and incantations recited during rituals.

In addition to water, other natural elements played a crucial role in healing rituals. Incense, for example, was not just a pleasant fragrance that filled temples and homes. It was a spiritual vehicle, a means by which prayers and invocations ascended to the heavens. Incense purified the environment and created a protective barrier against evil influences that could impede the healing process. It was common for fumigations to be performed around the sick, with the purpose of warding off evil spirits and negative energies that could be causing or prolonging the illness.

Amulets were also used extensively, with a purpose far beyond the ornamental. They functioned as conductors of spiritual energies, projecting protection and healing to those who wore them. Each amulet was chosen based on the illness or the protection needed. The Eye of Horus, for example, was widely used in healing rituals for its symbolism of restoration and protection. The use of such amulets was accompanied by incantations that activated their power, ensuring that the individual remained safe and under the protection of the gods.

The priest-doctors, in addition to mastering magic, also used a variety of natural substances that had recognized healing properties. Medicinal plants were used in ointments, poultices, and potions, and their effects were enhanced by magic and rituals. Among the most commonly used substances were garlic, known for its antiseptic properties, and myrrh, which was used in healing and embalming procedures. The priests understood that these substances, in combination with divine intervention, could restore health and vitality to patients.

One of the most impressive rituals regarding healing was the use of "waters of life", a sacred liquid prepared inside temples and imbued with magical energy. These waters were applied to the sick person's body or ingested as part of the treatment, and it was believed that they carried with them the vital energy necessary to revitalize the body and expel the disease. In many cases, this ritual was accompanied by songs and dances, performed by dedicated priestesses, who believed they could channel the energy of the gods directly to the patient.

Finally, the role of priest-doctors in the healing process went beyond the mere administration of treatments. They acted as mediators between the patient and the gods, guiding the sick person through the process of spiritual healing. The patient often went through a process of spiritual purification, where they confessed their faults or imbalances that could have caused their condition. This process of introspection and repentance was fundamental to restoring ma'at within the individual, creating the path to physical renewal.

Thus, the Egyptian healing rituals not only treated the body but restored the spiritual order, where every word, every gesture, and every element of nature was used to reconnect the patient with the divine force.

Chapter 3
Rituals of Prosperity and Abundance

For the ancient Egyptians, prosperity was a gift from the gods, a manifestation of divine benevolence that kept life in balance and order. At the heart of this quest for abundance were rituals dedicated to ensuring the fertility of the land, abundance in harvests, and protection against pests that threatened the livelihood of families. The connection to the land was deep, and the cycle of the seasons, closely linked to the movement of the Nile, guided life and rituals. In each phase, the gods were called upon to ensure that chaos, isfet, was kept at bay and that harmony, ma'at, governed natural forces and social life.

Osiris, the god of vegetation and the afterlife, was one of the central figures when it came to prosperity and abundance. It was believed that his death and resurrection symbolized the eternal cycle of harvests and the regeneration of life. In the annual festivals celebrated in his honor, there were rituals that involved symbolic sowing, where small statues of Osiris were buried in fertile land, representing the planting of life and the cyclical renewal of nature. Throughout the year, the god was revered with offerings, prayers, and ceremonies, to ensure that abundance returned and that the soil continued to bear fruit.

Hapi, the god of the Nile, was another powerful symbol of prosperity. The Nile, being the beating heart of Egypt, with its annual floods that brought fertile silt to the banks of the river, was seen as a divine gift. Control of the Nile's waters was essential to ensure good harvests, and, as such, Hapi was often revered with offerings during the Flood festival. During this period, the river, swollen by the rains, was greeted with songs and gifts, such as fruits, flowers, and small symbolic boats, launched into its waters in gratitude and supplication for a year of abundance.

The rituals to ensure prosperity were not only dedicated to collective well-being but also to individual abundance. To attract luck and ensure success in harvests or trade, many families made private offerings in their homes or small sanctuaries. Fruits, breads, and incense were offered to the gods of fertility and wealth, such as Renenutet, the goddess of harvests, who was seen as a protector of crops and agricultural wealth. These private rituals were an extension of what happened in temples, bringing the power of the gods into everyday life.

The act of offering generously to the gods was seen as a reflection of divine abundance itself. The more a person or community gave to the gods, the more they received in return. The concept of reciprocity was fundamental. Offerings were not just gestures of devotion but spiritual investments that sought to ensure return in the form of abundance. This practice was rooted in the belief that the gods controlled every aspect of nature, from the growth of crops to protection from storms and pests. Therefore, offerings served to maintain this healthy relationship between humans and divinities, where both depended on each other to sustain the order of the world.

In temples, offerings were part of carefully choreographed rituals, where priests, acting on behalf of the pharaoh and the people, brought the fruits of the earth to the feet of the gods. In ceremonies involving songs and processions, the priests carried baskets full of grains, fruits, flowers, and bread, presenting these gifts as a symbol of human gratitude and a request for continued protection and prosperity. The very architecture of the temples reflected this concern with fertility and abundance. Many temples, such as Karnak, had corridors lined with sphinxes and gardens that symbolized the vitality and generosity of the land.

At the center of these rituals was the belief that earthly life was an extension of divine life. Every action, every offering, and every prayer had a direct impact on physical reality, shaping the conditions of life on earth. The rituals of prosperity were, therefore, a means of ensuring that the gods continued to pour their blessings on the people, maintaining ma'at and warding off isfet, which could manifest as famine, pests, or natural disasters.

The festival of the Nile, one of the most anticipated celebrations on the Egyptian calendar, was a time when all the people united in a single purpose: to ensure that the waters rose at the right time and in the right amount. During this festival, the Egyptians gathered on the banks of the river, offering gifts in pottery and praying to Hapi for the flood to be abundant, but not devastating. They believed that divine intervention controlled the flow of the waters, and so every gesture, from the songs to the objects offered to the river, was performed with an almost solemn reverence.

The annual festivities were not limited to Hapi and the Nile. The Egyptian agricultural cycle was punctuated by various sacred events, where different gods were invoked to protect and ensure the success of each phase of the agricultural process. From planting to harvest, ceremonies were adjusted to ensure that the natural cycle was respected and that the fertility of the land was not compromised. At these times, collective participation reinforced the idea that the prosperity of an individual was intertwined with the prosperity of the community, and that together, they could influence the gods in their favor.

These rituals of prosperity and abundance, deeply rooted in the daily lives of the Egyptians, were an expression of the belief that everything in life depended on the harmony between the human and divine worlds. Through offerings, prayers, and festivities, the Egyptian people sought to ensure that the flow of life continued, without interruption, in an eternal dance between heaven and earth.

The celebrations dedicated to prosperity were not limited to isolated moments but were part of a continuous cycle, where each ritual had its place in the natural flow of the seasons and the needs of daily life. Throughout the year, the Egyptians performed a series of ceremonies to ensure that the blessings of the gods continued to flow, not only on their crops but on all aspects of their lives: from the well-being of families to success in commercial endeavors.

The annual festival of Opet, one of the grandest celebrations of ancient Thebes, was one of the times when the prosperity of the kingdom was reaffirmed on a divine scale. During this ceremony, the god Amun-Ra, in his form as creator and sustainer of order, was transported from the temple of Karnak to the temple of Luxor in a grand procession that included priests, musicians, dancers, and fervent crowds. The gods were carried in sacred boats, symbolically sailing the Nile, which reinforced the link between the river, fertility, and the prosperity of Egypt.

The belief in the power of rituals to ensure abundance was also seen in the consecration of objects and work tools, especially during preparations for planting and harvesting. Before the farmer sowed the seeds in the ground, it was common for him to perform small blessing rituals on his tools, asking the gods to favor the work and protect the land from pests. These rituals, although private and often performed far from temples, were fundamental to the Egyptians, who knew that even the most mundane tasks depended on divine favor.

The temples, in turn, not only housed the statues of the gods but also functioned as centers for the redistribution of resources. It was believed that, through the abundant offerings made in the temples, the divinities redistributed their blessings in the form of material prosperity. This occurred both on the spiritual and physical levels: the surplus of offerings was often used to feed the priests and temple workers, creating a cycle where the gifts offered to the gods returned to the community.

Among the most important rituals dedicated to prosperity was the practice of continuous offerings. These offerings, made regularly and according to the religious calendar, consisted of valuables, food, and flowers that were brought to the gods as a demonstration of devotion and gratitude. In the temple of Ra, for example, the priests performed daily offering rites, in which bread, beer, and meat were offered in large quantities, symbolizing the abundance that Ra provided by maintaining the cycle of day and night.

These ceremonies were not restricted to the elites. In times of great festivity, the general population participated in the celebrations, bringing their own offerings to the gods. During the most important festivities, such as the Nile flood festival, crowds gathered on the banks of the river to thank the gods and ask for another year of abundance. There, small boats laden with flowers and fruits were launched into the waters, symbolizing total surrender to the natural flow of life, trusting that the gods would return in abundance what had been offered to them.

The role of women in prosperity rituals was equally significant. Often associated with the goddess Hathor, they actively participated in ceremonies aimed at abundance, not only in large festivities but also in domestic rituals. Hathor, goddess of music, fertility, and joy, was invoked to ensure happiness in homes and prosperity in families. In her sanctuaries, women sang, danced, and offered drinks and food, asking for her protection and blessings so that their children would grow strong and healthy and that their husbands would be successful in their work.

The consecration of objects was another crucial aspect of prosperity rituals. Many items, from agricultural implements to personal amulets, were blessed in specific ceremonies to ensure that they were imbued with the divine energy needed to attract good luck. Amulets, such as the Ankh - symbol of life - and the Scarab - symbol of rebirth and transformation - were common in these rites. These objects not only brought protection but also acted as conductors of cosmic energy, ensuring that those who carried them were constantly enveloped by the forces of prosperity.

The annual ceremonies of ancient Egypt, aimed at guaranteeing abundance, were not limited to agricultural matters. The celebrations of the festival of Min, the god of male fertility and harvests, for example, included rituals of a sexual and symbolic nature, intended to promote the fecundity of the land and the people. During these celebrations, the statues of Min were adorned with lettuce leaves, a plant considered an aphrodisiac, and large processions were held in which people sang and danced in honor of the god, asking him to ensure fertility for the next agricultural cycle.

Prosperity, however, was not just a matter of harvests or material wealth. For the Egyptians, true abundance also included social harmony and political stability. Specific rituals were performed to ensure that the pharaoh, as the highest representative of ma'at, could continue to rule with wisdom and justice, guaranteeing peace in the kingdom and prosperity for all. These rituals involved the active participation of the pharaoh, who presented himself before the gods in the temples, making offerings on behalf of all the people and reaffirming his commitment to the cosmic order.

Individual prosperity practices were also of great importance. Personal amulets, such as the Eye of Horus or the knot of Isis, were worn as talismans of protection and attraction of good luck. These sacred objects were carried during daily activities and in times of uncertainty, such as on business trips or land negotiations. The belief was that by carrying a piece of divine power with them, the person would be protected from misfortunes and blessed with success and fortune.

These rituals, which connected the divine to the everyday, showed how the Egyptians saw prosperity as a state that could be cultivated through right actions and constant devotion to the gods. Through collective ceremonies and personal rituals, the Egyptian people perpetuated a continuous relationship with the divine forces, ensuring that the flow of life remained harmonious and prosperous, in keeping with the eternal cycles of nature and the cosmos.

Chapter 4
Rituals of Connection with the Gods

In the vastness of the Egyptian desert, where the sun scorched the horizon and the wind whispered ancient tales, there existed a profound belief in spiritual ascension. For the Egyptians, life on Earth was but a fraction of existence, and the connection with the divine world, the path to the gods, was a destiny desired by all. However, only those who prepared themselves adequately, through complex and intense rituals, could hope to achieve this elevated state of union with the deities. The pharaohs, in particular, held a privileged role in this process, as their lives were seen as constant preparation for a divine ascension after death.

The rituals that promoted this ascension began long before the end of physical life. They involved continuous purification, both of the body and the spirit. The practice of ritual baths, often performed in sacred waters, was part of this preparation, cleansing not only physical impurities but also spiritual ones. Priests conducted these rites, invoking the presence of gods such as Horus and Isis, guides of spiritual transition, to prepare the individual for the encounter with the divine. Ritual garments, made of pure linen, reinforced the symbolism of purity, warding off impure energies and surrounding the practitioner with the light of the gods.

Meditation also occupied an essential place in the rituals of spiritual ascension. Through it, the initiate sought to access higher dimensions of existence, where the human mind could connect with cosmic energies. These moments of deep introspection were often accompanied by chants and incantations, recited in low voices by the priests, creating an environment where the physical world slowly dissolved, allowing consciousness to expand. The Egyptians believed that by reaching elevated states of meditation, it was possible to approach the gods, receiving visions and wisdom directly from the spiritual plane.

Within the sacred temples, the ascension ritual also involved constant offerings. Food, incense, and precious objects were offered to the statues of the gods, which represented their earthly manifestations. These rituals were intended to open the channels of communication between the devotee and the divine, allowing the power of the gods to flow into the physical world. Offerings were seen as a way to nourish the gods, ensuring their protection and spiritual guidance for the practitioner. The sound of the sistrum, a sacred instrument of Hathor, echoed through the temple corridors, intensifying the mystical atmosphere and inviting divine forces to actively participate in the ritual.

At the heart of these rituals was the desire to transcend physical reality. For the Egyptians, the body was only a temporary vehicle, a shell that, over time, wore out. The spirit, however, was eternal, and the ultimate goal of life was to ensure that, upon leaving the physical body, the spirit was prepared to ascend to the realms of the gods. The pharaohs, in particular, were prepared for this journey with special rigor. It was believed that upon death, the pharaoh transformed into a god, joining the divine pantheon to guide and protect Egypt from higher dimensions.

One of the most mysterious and powerful moments in the process of spiritual ascension involved the incorporation of the gods. Sacred texts, such as the "Pyramid Texts," detailed complex rituals that allowed the essence of a god to be invoked and embodied by a pharaoh or priest. During these ceremonies, the initiate became a channel through which the gods could manifest in the physical world. It was a dangerous and sacred process, requiring absolute spiritual purity and deep mental control. The incorporation not only strengthened the individual's connection with the gods but also ensured that they were ready to join them at the moment of their final passage.

The rituals of spiritual ascension were, in essence, a journey of self-discovery and transformation. The initiate, by purifying themselves and connecting with the divine, experienced a symbolic death of the ego and the physical body, allowing their true spiritual essence to emerge. This rebirth was celebrated with sacred songs and dances, symbolizing the victory of spirit over matter, and the final union with the cosmos.

The ceremonies that sought spiritual ascension in ancient Egypt were not just earthly practices, but profound journeys into the mystery of the divine.

Performed in temples that echoed with the weight of millennia of sacred wisdom, these rituals were designed to bring initiates closer to higher forces, allowing them, through a gradual process, to merge with the gods. The temples, with their imposing columns, dark chambers, and secret corridors, were more than physical constructions: they were spiritual passages that guided participants to the realm of the gods, where time and space intertwined in an incomprehensible way.

In the recesses of these sacred chambers, only high-ranking priests and pharaohs had access to the most complex rituals of divine incorporation. The deep silence was broken only by the sound of the chanted songs, words that reverberated on the stone walls like echoes of bygone eras, charged with an ancient power. The use of pyramid texts, carefully inscribed in royal tombs and on papyri, detailed the invocations and incantations that allowed connection with the gods. These texts were much more than instructions; they contained spiritual formulas that guided the initiate on their journey, protecting their soul from the forces of chaos and guiding them towards enlightenment.

The process of spiritual ascension, however, required more than the mere recitation of incantations or ritual offerings. The initiate needed to undergo a series of intense purifications, both internal and external. In the case of the pharaohs, the rituals began while they were still alive, with renewal ceremonies that symbolized the eternal cycle of death and rebirth. One such practice involved the symbolic reenactment of the journey of Osiris, the god of resurrection. Osiris, killed and dismembered, was restored and elevated by the magic of Isis, his wife. For the Egyptians, this story was not just a myth, but a cosmic truth that every soul needed to experience in order to achieve ascension.

Inside the pyramids, the ascension rituals reached their peak. The pyramids, precisely aligned with the stars, especially the constellation of Orion and the star Sirius, functioned as conductors of cosmic energy. It was believed that, upon death, the pharaoh's spirit ascended to heaven through these sacred alignments, guided by the enchantments engraved on the inner walls. These texts not only described the path of the soul but also functioned as protective shields, ensuring that the spirit was received in the realm of the gods without being diverted by negative forces.

The role of the priests in this process was vitally important. They were the guardians of spiritual secrets, the only ones with the necessary knowledge to interpret and perform the rituals correctly. Each gesture, each word uttered, had a deep meaning. A wrong move or a cursed word could compromise the journey of the pharaoh or initiate. Thus, priests were trained throughout their lives to master these ceremonies, carrying the weight of millennia of tradition in their hands and voices. Their bodies, often adorned with amulets and sacred vestments, became channels through which divine energy flowed.

Another fascinating aspect of these rituals was the use of enchantments to achieve altered states of consciousness. The initiate, be it pharaoh or priest, went through long periods of isolation, where their mind and spirit were prepared to transcend physical reality. The process involved fasting, deep meditation, and sometimes the use of sacred substances that amplified spiritual perceptions. In these ceremonies, the mind was freed from the shackles of the body, allowing the initiate to journey beyond the visible world, toward the stars and the cosmos.

Upon reaching a state of spiritual ecstasy, the initiate experienced the direct presence of the gods. In some cases, it was believed that the initiate's own spirit could temporarily merge with that of a deity, allowing them to experience the reality of the divine world. These experiences were seen as moments of supreme enlightenment, where the initiate transcended time and space and understood the deep secrets of creation. Ecstasy was not merely an emotional experience; it was a mystical union with cosmic forces, where the individual became part of ma'at, the universal order that sustained life.

However, spiritual ascension was not the end of the journey. For the Egyptians, this connection with the gods also brought with it a greater responsibility. The initiate, now transformed and purified, needed to return to the physical world with a deeper understanding of their role in the cosmos. The pharaoh, in particular, having experienced union with the gods, reassumed his role as maintainer of divine order on Earth. Each rite of spiritual ascension was, therefore, a renewal of the covenant between man and the gods, a reaffirmation that the balance of the universe depended on this sacred relationship.

These rituals of spiritual ascension and connection with the gods, with their complexity and depth, were more than religious practices. They represented the core of Egyptian spirituality, where life and death, body and spirit, were intertwined in an eternal cosmic dance. Through these rituals, the Egyptians sought not only to understand the universe, but to unite with it, transcending what was mortal and ephemeral, to become part of the eternal divine cycle.

Chapter 5
Rituals for Victory in Battles and Conflicts

Before the clang of swords and the rumble of war chariots across the sands of Egypt, there was a moment of sacred silence. It was in this interval, between calm and chaos, that the Egyptians invoked the power of the gods to ensure victory. The deep belief that battles were won not only by earthly strategies but by the intervention of divine forces permeated every conflict. War, for them, was an extension of the eternal struggle between ma'at, order, and isfet, chaos. Thus, before any military campaign, solemn rituals were performed to ensure that the cosmic balance was on Egypt's side.

Horus, the falcon-headed god, symbol of power and protection, was one of the most frequently invoked deities. It was believed that he, as the avenger of his father Osiris, granted strength and courage to those who defended justice. The pharaoh, considered a living embodiment of Horus, led the ceremonies, not only as a military commander but as a spiritual intermediary between the gods and the armies. On the eve of battles, he would make offerings of food and incense, while uttering invocations that Horus would give him keen vision and dexterity to defeat his enemies.

Montu, the fierce god of war, was another protector of the Egyptian forces. His cult was particularly strong in Thebes, where he was seen as the god who personified the impetus of battle. In the temples dedicated to Montu, the pharaoh and his priests conducted weapon consecration rituals. Bronze blades, bows, shields and spears were carefully anointed with sacred oils, while words of power were chanted to imbue these objects with divine strength and protection. It was believed that by consecrating weapons, they became extensions of the gods, instruments of ma'at against the forces of chaos.

Each Egyptian soldier, before marching into battle, carried amulets of protection. The eye of Horus, the udjat, was common among warriors, considered a spiritual shield that warded off curses and guided the soldier during combat. Amulets of Bes, the little protector god, were also popular among the troops. Although Bes was commonly associated with domestic protection and children, he was also seen as a force that warded off evil in all its forms. In war, he became a fierce guardian, protecting soldiers from imminent danger.

The ceremonies that preceded the fighting were not limited to the pharaoh and the warriors. Temples throughout Egypt resounded with prayers and chants as priests invoked divine protection over the army. High on the temple towers, statues of Horus and Montu were erected so that their presence would bless the troops. Offerings of animals, such as bulls and birds, were made to the warrior gods, asking them to ensure success on the battlefield and bring the army back unharmed.

In addition to weapons, the warriors themselves were consecrated. Priests passed through the ranks of soldiers, touching them with branches of sacred plants, such as myrrh and papyrus, while murmuring incantations of protection and strength. This symbolic blessing was seen as an invisible armor that would protect the soldier from blows and curses. Upon receiving this blessing, each warrior felt not only physically prepared, but spiritually strengthened, believing that the presence of the gods would accompany him in battle.

A crucial practice during war rituals was the consecration of standards. The flags and banners of the Egyptian troops, which bore the sacred symbols of the gods, were considered foci of divine power. Before each campaign, priests purified these standards with incense smoke and prayers, imbuing them with the energy of the gods they represented. When troops advanced with these symbols, they felt guided by the strength of Horus, Montu, or Amun-Ra himself, whose spiritual presence was ensured through the standard.

The prayers and incantations spoken before battles were not just to ensure victory. There was also an aspect of spiritual protection for the warriors, preventing their souls from being claimed by chaos should they lose their lives on the battlefield. The Egyptians believed that death in combat, if not properly protected by the gods, could open the way for the souls of warriors to be lost in the underworld. Therefore, in addition to praying for an earthly victory, the ceremonies also asked that the souls of the soldiers, should they fall, be received by Osiris and find rest in the afterlife.

These rituals, performed before battles, were both physical and spiritual preparation. While the army equipped itself and prepared for the clash, the soul of each warrior was attuned to the strength of the gods. The ceremonies not only served to invoke divine protection, but also to remind the soldiers that their causes were just, and that, as defenders of ma'at, they had the right and duty to win. The battlefield was seen not only as a place of physical confrontation, but as a sacred territory where order and chaos clashed, and the gods, summoned by rituals, decided the fate of each combat.

War, in ancient Egypt, did not end with the last blow struck on the battlefield. Victory, even if achieved with the favor of the gods, required closing rituals, not only to honor the conquest, but to restore order in the hearts and souls of the warriors. After the return of the victorious troops, it was necessary to thank the deities for the protection granted and to perform purification ceremonies so that the chaos, released during combat, was contained and dispelled.

Post-battle enchantments, known for their spiritual power, had the function of ensuring that the forces of chaos, always present in wars, were definitively subdued. These rituals, often performed in the great temples of Karnak or Luxor, began with prayers in honor of Montu and Horus, warrior gods, who had guided the army to victory. The priests, in long processions, carried sacred banners through the streets, proclaiming that victory belonged not only to men, but also to the gods who had blessed them.

Animal sacrifices, especially bulls, were performed in honor of the war gods as a form of gratitude. The blood shed in these sacrifices did not symbolize violence, but life, the renewed cycle of divine order. These intensely symbolic rituals served to strengthen the bond between the pharaoh, the army, and the deities. The pharaohs, as representatives of the gods on Earth, also participated directly in these rituals, offering the first sacrifices themselves, connecting their military victories with the renewal of ma'at, the cosmic order.

Another crucial aspect of post-conflict rituals was the purification of warriors. After having shed blood in combat, even if victorious, soldiers needed to free themselves from the spiritual impurities acquired during the confrontation. War was seen as a manifestation of chaos, and those who participated in it needed to purify themselves in order to return to civilian life without carrying the spiritual marks of destruction. Ritual baths in the sacred waters of the Nile, accompanied by prayers from priests, were performed to wash away the energies of conflict and allow warriors to return to their homes in peace.

The consecration of weapons, such an important ritual before battle, also needed to be reversed. Weapons used in combat, impregnated by the chaos of war, were returned to temples to be purified. Priests immersed them in sacred waters, while chanting purification songs, removing from them the energy of confrontation.

The blades were polished again, not only to restore their physical appearance but to erase the energies accumulated during the war. This process was essential, as any tool that bore the mark of chaos could not be used again until it was purified, or it could bring imbalance to the home of the bearer.

Post-war rituals also included tributes to the dead, both allies and enemies. The Egyptians had a deep respect for the souls of those who perished, and believed that even enemies, if fallen in combat, needed to be honored so that their souls would not disturb ma'at. Funeral ceremonies were performed for fallen warriors, in which offerings of food and flowers were made to the gods of death, such as Osiris and Anubis, to ensure that these souls found their safe passage to the underworld. For Egyptian soldiers, this meant being received in the realm of Osiris, where they could live in eternal peace in the field of reeds.

The bodies of allied warriors were carefully embalmed, following traditional funeral rituals, which ensured the preservation of the body and the safe passage of the soul. In the case of enemies, their bodies were returned to their lands of origin, or, in some cases, simplified purification ceremonies were performed to ensure that their souls did not wander the desert, disturbing the living. This respect for the dead, regardless of their role in the conflict, was a reflection of the Egyptian belief that everyone deserved a peaceful journey to the afterlife.

Victory celebrations also involved festivals and banquets, where the Egyptian people united in festivities to honor the gods and celebrate the return of the warriors. Wine, bread and meat, which had been offered in small portions during the war, were now consumed in abundance, a clear demonstration that prosperity had been restored with victory. The priests participated in these festivities, blessing the food and wine, ensuring that the celebrations maintained a sacred character.

An important moment in the post-conflict ritual was the "land purification" ceremony. After a battle, the battlefield was considered contaminated by the energies of chaos and death. Priests were sent to the battlefields to perform purification rites. Small statues of protective deities, such as Bastet and Anubis, were buried in the ground, while chants and offerings of incense and flowers were made to restore harmony to the land. This ritual was essential to ensure that chaos did not remain at the battle site and that the fertility of the land was maintained.

Finally, the standards that had led the Egyptian armies to victory were taken back to the temples, where they were purified and consecrated again. These symbols, which represented the power of the gods, received special offerings of gold and incense, and remained stored in the temples until they were summoned again for another conflict. These standards, although they carried the energy of war, were also seen as powerful amulets that ensured the continued victory of Egypt.

Post-war rituals were, therefore, a complex process of transition, where the chaos of battle was transformed back into order. Egypt, protected by the gods and sacred rituals, returned to the state of harmony that defined its relationship with the cosmos, ensuring that victory in the field was not only physical, but spiritual and eternal.

Chapter 6
Rituals of Protection and Spiritual Defense

Ancient Egypt was enveloped by invisible forces that acted upon the physical and spiritual world. For the Egyptians, the universe was permeated by energies and entities, many of which could be both protective and threatening. Protection against these invisible dangers was not just a matter of physical self-defense, but of maintaining *ma'at* - the cosmic balance - in all aspects of life. And it was with this belief that the Egyptians developed complex rituals of protection, which included the use of amulets, incantations, and the invocation of guardian deities, such as Bastet and Anubis.

At the center of Egyptian spiritual life, protection was a sacred concept. The forces of chaos, always present and always ready to invade the established order, were combated through rituals involving gestures, words, and objects of power. Spiritual protection began in the personal sphere. Each individual, whether noble or peasant, believed in the need to protect themselves from the evil influences that could interfere in their daily lives. And this belief was materialized through amulets, sacred objects that were believed to channel divine energy.

Among the best-known amulets was the famous *Udjat*, or the Eye of Horus. This powerful symbol was used to ward off negative energies and bring protection to both body and soul. The Eye of Horus represented totality and integrity, being one of the most popular among the Egyptians. Each time an Udjat amulet was carved or molded, it underwent a consecration ritual in the temple, where the priests invoked the energy of Horus to imbue the object with protective power. The bearer of the amulet, upon wearing it, felt enveloped by the presence of Horus, believing that the god was vigilant, warding off any evil that might approach.

Another widely used amulet was the scarab, which symbolized transformation and renewal. Although commonly associated with the afterlife, the scarab was also used as protection in earthly life. It was believed that this amulet, consecrated by priests with prayers and incantations, could protect the bearer from the evil forces that roamed the physical and spiritual world. In times of crisis, such as illness or attacks by enemies, Egyptians resorting to this amulet felt supported by the forces of creation and renewal that it represented.

Personal protection rituals also involved the use of incantations. These words of power were carefully preserved and passed down through generations by priests, who held deep knowledge of the power of words in the spiritual world. It was believed that words, when spoken correctly, had the power to shape reality. In times of greatest danger, both physical and spiritual, the Egyptians resorted to these sacred words to invoke divine protection. A simple incantation, when spoken in the right context and with due reverence, could ward off evil spirits and restore the energy balance of a person or place.

Among the most revered protective deities was Bastet, the lioness-headed goddess, who symbolized the protection of home and family. Bastet, although often portrayed as a peaceful and maternal goddess, also had a fierce side, capable of warding off any threat with her strength and determination. Her temples, especially in Bubastis, were places of intense worship, where people brought offerings in exchange for her protection. When invoked in rituals, Bastet was called upon to protect the home, ward off malicious spirits, and ensure the safety of all family members. In Egyptian homes, small statues of Bastet were placed in prominent places, surrounded by offerings of incense and flowers, to ensure her protective presence.

Anubis, the jackal-headed god, was also a figure of extreme importance when it came to spiritual protection. Although best known for his role as guardian of the dead, Anubis was equally invoked to protect the living from spiritual dangers. His dominion over the world of the dead made him a powerful deity to ward off wandering spirits and evil forces that roamed between the two worlds. In rituals, the symbol of Anubis was often inscribed on amulets and portals to ensure that no evil force could cross. The priests, knowledgeable in funerary practices and the secrets of Anubis, performed ceremonies in which they invoked his power to ensure that the soul and body were always protected, both in life and in death.

Protection was not limited to the individual, but also to the physical space that surrounded them. Egyptian homes, especially those of the most devout families, were consecrated with rituals of protection, where doors and windows received amulets and inscriptions of enchantments. Sacred incenses, like *kyphi*, were burned regularly, their smoke rising like an invisible shield against any negative energy that might try to penetrate the home. These domestic rituals were an extension of the practices performed in the temples, but with a more intimate and personal focus.

In addition to physical objects and incantations, protection rituals often involved symbolic gestures. One of the oldest and most powerful gestures was that of the outstretched hand, a symbol of defense against the forces of evil. Represented in paintings and engravings, this gesture was performed during specific rituals, where the priest, upon raising his hand, symbolized the spiritual barrier against any invisible threat. These gestures, accompanied by sacred words, amplified the power of the ritual, creating a barrier between the physical world and spiritual dangers.

Personal protection rituals were, therefore, more than just traditions. They were a daily practice that reflected the Egyptian understanding that the spiritual world was in constant interaction with the physical world. Protecting oneself from these invisible influences was to ensure the continuity of life, harmony and *ma'at*, which, for the Egyptians, was essential to maintain the balance of the cosmos and inner peace.

Protection in ancient Egypt went beyond the individual and the family, extending to the community and even the nation. Spiritual threats were seen as real dangers, capable of affecting not only people's health, but also social and political stability. The Egyptians believed that Egypt itself, with its temples and fertile fields, needed a robust spiritual defense to maintain *ma'at* - the cosmic order that governed all things. Thus, complex rituals were developed to protect villages, cities, and, in critical moments, the kingdom itself against destructive forces, be they spiritual or physical.

One of the most powerful collective rituals to protect entire communities was the creation of protective talismans. These talismans were often carved in stone or metal and placed in strategic locations, such as the gates of a city or the entrances to temples. Statues of gods such as Anubis, Bastet, and Ra were common in these practices, each imbued with spiritual power through specific rituals performed by priests. These talismans were intended to prevent evil spirits and destructive forces from crossing the physical and spiritual boundaries of the city.

One of the grandest rituals involving collective spiritual protection was performed at the Opet festival in Thebes. This event, in addition to celebrating the renewal of the pharaoh's power, included rituals aimed at protecting the city and the empire. During the festival, statues of the gods Amun, Mut, and Khonsu were carried in processions that crossed the Nile, linking the temple of Karnak to the temple of Luxor. The power of these deities, invoked with chants and offerings, was directed to protect the land and the people. It was believed that, by completing this cycle, divine energy reinvigorated not only the pharaoh, but also Egypt itself, erecting a spiritual barrier against any threats.

The priests, who were the guardians of sacred knowledge, played a central role in these collective protection rituals. In times of crisis, such as excessive floods or droughts, they were called upon to perform ceremonies to restore balance between the people and the gods. Temples were flooded with offerings, and prayers were recited incessantly, invoking the gods to ward off natural disasters and bring fertility back to the land. Complex rituals, such as "Sealing Chaos", involved the creation of magic circles around cities, in which priests traced powerful symbols on the ground, invoking the power of protective deities to block the forces of *isfet*.

The cycle of the seasons also brought with it spiritual threats, especially during the transitions between winter and summer. At these times, the Egyptians believed that the veil between the physical and spiritual worlds became thinner, allowing evil entities to approach. To combat these influences, seasonal festivals were held in various cities, where specific gods were invoked to restore balance. At the festival of Bastet, for example, thousands of devotees traveled to Bubastis, where they celebrated the goddess with music, dance, and offerings. The power of Bastet, invoked in these festivities, not only protected families and communities, but also warded off bad luck and diseases that could arise during the changing seasons.

Collective protection also involved ceremonies performed in times of war. When Egypt was under threat of invasion, spiritual protection rituals for the kingdom were performed in the most sacred chambers of the temples. The pharaoh, as the intermediary between the gods and men, led these rituals, where precious offerings, such as gold and incense, were presented to the warrior gods. Anubis, Horus, and Montu were invoked to form an invisible shield around Egypt's borders, protecting the land from invaders. It was believed that the gods, once satisfied with the offerings, would erect impenetrable spiritual barriers, ensuring that *ma'at* prevailed over the chaos brought by enemies.

Another essential ritual for collective protection was the "Disaster Warding Festival." During this festival, held annually, the priests, accompanied by community members, led processions that passed through the streets of the cities. These processions carried statues of protective gods, which were taken to the edges of the city to create a spiritual barrier against destructive forces, such as plagues and famines. The smoke of incense perfumed the air, while sacred chants echoed through the alleys and squares, raising prayers to the gods. The festival not only offered physical and spiritual protection, but also strengthened the bonds between the residents and the temples, reinforcing the belief that Egypt's security depended on the continued devotion and harmony between gods and men.

In addition to large ceremonies, the Egyptians also performed smaller but powerful rituals to protect their lands from curses and disasters. Amulets and small talismans were buried in agricultural fields, accompanied by prayers to Renenutet, the goddess of the harvest, asking her to ward off pests and ensure good harvests. These agricultural protection rituals were especially important in rural communities, where life depended on the bounty of the land. The use of sacred animal figures, such as snakes and cats, was common in these rituals, as these animals were seen as natural defenders of the forces of life and guardians against chaos.

Collective spiritual defenses were not limited to protecting the present, but also ensured the protection of the future. In critical moments, priests performed rituals of divination and communication with the gods to ensure that *ma'at* was maintained for future generations. Through oracles and divine signs, they sought guidance on how to avoid disasters and ensure the continuity of Egypt's prosperity. These rituals reinforced the belief that, although the future was uncertain, the gods, when properly invoked and revered, would continue to protect the land and its people against any form of threat, visible or invisible.

Thus, collective protection rituals in Egypt were not just spiritual practices, but a manifestation of the deep connection between the people, their land, and the cosmos. Each city, each temple, each home, was a reflection of the cosmic order that needed to be maintained. The Egyptians understood that true security came from maintaining this order, through devotion and respect for rituals that kept chaos at bay and preserved harmony in all aspects of life.

Chapter 7
Rituals of Life Renewal

Fertility, for the ancient Egyptians, was a sacred force that permeated all spheres of existence. Life, in its essence, depended on the constant cycle of birth, growth, and renewal. This eternal dance between beginning and beginning again found an echo in the surrounding nature, in the waters of the Nile that brought fertile mud, in the seeds that germinated, and in the births that perpetuated the continuity of humanity. And, to ensure that this cycle was never interrupted, the Egyptians resorted to elaborate rituals that invoked the energy of powerful deities, such as Isis and Hathor, whose powers encompassed both human and agricultural fertility.

In many of the temples scattered along the Nile, Isis was revered as the Great Mother, the one who, with her wisdom and magic, ensured the continuity of life. The figure of Isis, goddess of motherhood and fertility, was invoked in fertility rituals to ensure that women conceived healthy children and to bless mothers who were already pregnant. At the altars dedicated to Isis, priestesses made offerings of milk and honey, symbols of nutrition and life, while prayers were chanted asking for her intervention. It was believed that, through these rites, women could receive the strength of Isis, increasing their chances of generating new life.

Fertility, however, was not restricted to the womb of women. The soil, the basis of Egypt's survival, also needed the blessing of the gods to remain fertile. For this, Hathor, goddess of joy, love, and fertility, was often invoked. The seasonal rituals dedicated to Hathor, performed before and after harvests, were intended to ensure that the Egyptian lands continued to produce abundance. Small statues of Hathor were buried on the banks of the fields, accompanied by offerings of fruits, flowers, and grains, symbolizing renewal and the desire for abundance. These rituals reinforced the spiritual connection between the land and the gods, ensuring that the cycle of harvests remained prosperous.

In more intimate rituals, performed within Egyptian homes, women wore sacred amulets known as the "knot of Isis," which symbolized female life force. These amulets, consecrated by priests, were used as talismans of protection and fertility, and it is believed that women who wore them during pregnancy would be under the direct protection of the goddess. The power of these amulets was reinforced with incantations and prayers, which were repeated regularly, ensuring that the strength of Isis was always present.

In many villages and communities, fertility rituals involved not only the invocation of goddesses but also purification practices, intended to prepare the body and spirit for the arrival of new life. The use of sacred water, taken from springs or from the Nile itself, was common in these ceremonies. Pregnant women, in particular, underwent ritual baths, which were accompanied by prayers and sacred chants, asking not only for fertility but also for protection for the fetus. Water, a fundamental element of creation, was seen as a bearer of divine power, capable of cleansing and revitalizing both the physical and spiritual body.

In villages and large cities, celebrations in honor of the fertility of the land often involved processions carrying icons of Isis and Hathor through the fields. Priests and priestesses, accompanied by the people, performed chants and carried baskets of offerings that symbolized the desire for renewal. These moments were full of joy and devotion, as families gave thanks for past harvests and begged for abundance in those to come. It was believed that these processions and sacred chants opened a direct channel of communication with the goddesses, reinforcing the link between man and the divine.

Fertility rituals were not limited to invoking the blessing of the goddesses. They also involved a deep respect for the natural cycle of life. In times of drought or scarcity, when fertility seemed threatened, special rituals were performed to try to restore balance. During these ceremonies, priests invoked the presence of Hapi, the god of the Nile, asking him to bring the flood waters to nourish the dry lands and restore the fertility of the soil. The Nile, with its constant cycle of flooding and retraction, was seen as the very heart of Egypt, and the fertility of the land was directly linked to its generosity.

To ensure that the cycle of life continued, the Egyptians also performed rituals dedicated to the fertility of animals, which were crucial to the economy and the livelihood of families. Isis, as protector of animals, was invoked to bless the herds and ensure that livestock continued to reproduce and thrive. These rituals, often performed by shepherds and farmers, involved offerings of grain and milk, symbolizing the continuity of the natural cycle and the intimate relationship between the gods and life in the countryside.

Fertility, in all its aspects, was a vital force that united the Egyptians to the cosmos. And the rituals that invoked this force reflected the belief that, with the help of the gods, the cycle of life could be kept in balance. With each new birth, with each successful harvest, the Egyptians saw the renewal of the pact between man and the gods, where fertility was not just a blessing, but a sign that *ma'at* - the universal order - was in harmony with life.

The rhythm of the seasons, the cycle of harvests, and life itself were closely connected to fertility, and the Egyptians knew that to ensure continuity, they needed to honor the cosmic forces through seasonal rituals. The renewal of life, celebrated in ceremonies involving the community, was not just a request for prosperity, but a spiritual communion with the gods who governed the cycle of existence. Isis, Hathor, and other deities linked to fertility were invoked during these celebrations, as they were the ones who maintained the delicate balance between man, land, and animals.

The seasonal fertility ceremonies followed the flow of the Nile waters, which was Egypt's lifeblood.

When the river began to rise, flooding the banks and leaving behind fertile soil, the land was symbolically "reborn." At that moment, priests and priestesses performed rituals to consecrate the soil. They poured sacred water and uttered incantations invoking the blessing of Hapi, the god of the Nile, as the first seeds were sown. This ritualistic act was seen as a reenactment of the myth of creation, where fertility arose from primordial chaos, and life, once again, took shape.

Throughout the year, various community festivals were held to ensure the continuity of this fertility cycle. One of the most important was the Festival of Min, god of male fertility and vegetation. Min, often represented in his erect form, symbolized the life force that permeated nature and man. During his festival, images of the god were adorned with garlands of flowers, while priests held processions through the fields, invoking his strength to ensure abundant harvests. Lettuce, considered sacred to Min for its aphrodisiac properties, was used in offerings and consumed during rituals, reinforcing the connection between the god and the fertility of the land.

In addition to offerings, dance and music were also part of the seasonal rituals. People gathered in large celebrations, where music echoed through the fields, and ritual dances imitated the growth of plants and the rebirth of life. These dances were not just a manifestation of joy, but also a way of invoking the spiritual forces that guided the cycle of nature. The priestesses of Hathor, known for their dancing and singing skills, led these celebrations, believing that sound and movement could attract the divine presence and ensure continued fertility.

In the villages, during planting and harvesting, small altars were set up outdoors, where families brought simple offerings, such as bread, fruit, and flowers, in gratitude for the abundance. These rituals, although humble, were essential to maintain the bond between the people and the gods. Fertility amulets, such as the "knot of Isis" and the scarab, were often buried with the seeds, in the hope that their energies would ensure healthy growth of the crops. The land, seen as sacred, was treated with respect, and each symbolic gesture - from sowing to harvest - was a reflection of the people's devotion to the gods of fertility.

Fertility rituals, however, were not just related to land and animals. Human life itself was celebrated in a special way. In life renewal ceremonies, particularly after the birth of a child, the protective gods of children, such as Bes and Taweret, were invoked to ensure health and longevity for the newborn. Taweret, the hippopotamus-shaped goddess, was associated with childbirth and maternal protection. Her images were placed in homes to ward off the dangers of childbirth and ensure a prosperous and healthy life for children. These rituals of protection and blessing were performed both by priests in temples and by mothers in their homes, showing the depth of the Egyptian faith in the power of domestic rituals.

In the transition between seasons, especially at the end of the harvest, community rituals celebrated the complete cycle of life. These moments were an opportunity to thank the gods for their generosity and ask for protection for the next cycle. Families brought to the temples baskets of grain, fruit, and flowers, which were offered to the gods in a gesture of gratitude and devotion. These closing rituals of the agricultural cycle symbolized the constant renewal of life, where death and rebirth were intertwined.

At the end of the agricultural year, during the celebrations of Osiris, the god of death and resurrection, seeds were planted in small clay statues that represented the god. This gesture symbolized Osiris' power to restore life after death and ensure the eternal fertility of the land. The myth of Osiris, dismembered by Seth and restored by Isis, was revived in each ceremony, reinforcing the belief that death was only a phase of transition and that fertility, like life itself, continued in an eternal cycle of renewal.

These rituals, performed in temples and fields, were much more than just requests for abundance. They expressed the Egyptians' deep belief that the balance of life was in the hands of the gods and that, by maintaining this harmony through seasonal rituals and constant devotion, the renewal of life would be guaranteed. The land, animals, and humans were part of an interconnected whole, and the fertility of each depended on the spiritual connection with the divine forces that ruled the universe.

Thus, the renewal of life was not just a matter of survival, but a sacred dance between man, nature, and the gods. With each new season, the cycle repeated itself, renewing the pact between the Egyptians and the cosmos, where, through their rituals, they ensured that fertility never ceased to flow, and that life continued to sprout, like the waters of the Nile, infinitely.

Chapter 8
Rituals of Love and Union

For the ancient Egyptians, love was a sacred force that united not only bodies but also souls. Within the spiritual belief that permeated all spheres of life, rituals dedicated to love and marital union played an essential role in building and maintaining harmonious relationships. It was believed that love between individuals was blessed by the gods, especially Hathor, goddess of love, beauty, and music, and Isis, protector of women and marriages. The union between two people was seen not only as an earthly bond but as a spiritual connection that reverberated in the cosmic order.

Love and union rituals were performed both in temples and homes and involved a series of practices aimed at invoking divine blessings upon couples. When a couple wished to formalize their union, one of the first steps was to seek the approval of the gods. The couple, accompanied by family and priests, would go to the temples of Hathor or Isis, where offerings of flowers, perfumes, and food were deposited at the feet of the statues of these deities. These offerings symbolized the surrender of love and the marital relationship to divine care, ensuring that the marriage would be protected from negative influences.

Hathor, often depicted as a woman with cow ears or a solar disk on her head, was invoked to bring harmony, joy, and fertility to the couple. Her priestesses led chants and dances in honor of the goddess, while the couple received special amulets, which would guarantee the constant presence of Hathor in their relationship. These amulets, often in the shape of a heart symbol or an Eye of Horus, were consecrated in the temple and worn by the bride and groom as protection against envy and discord.

Egyptian marriage did not involve formal religious ceremonies like contemporary weddings, but the sacred rituals of consecrating love were deeply spiritual. The couple, before the statue of Hathor or Isis, asked for protection, fertility, and harmony. The priestesses, as intermediaries between the gods and mortals, performed silent prayers, invoking divine forces to seal the union. These rituals, shrouded in mystery, reinforced the belief that love, blessed by the deities, was an eternal, transcendent, and unbreakable force.

In addition to public rituals in temples, Egyptians also performed intimate ceremonies in their homes. On these occasions, small offerings were made to the gods of love in the family environment itself. Home altars, dedicated to Hathor or Isis, were decorated with flowers and incense, and the couple lit oil lamps, symbolizing the light of love that should guide their relationship. It was believed that by keeping the flame burning, the couple invoked the presence and protection of the deities, ensuring that love and happiness would perpetuate in the home.

The practice of union spells was also common among those seeking to strengthen love bonds or attract a loved one. These spells, which involved the use of amulets, enchantments, and potions, were performed by priests specializing in love magic. The enchantments generally involved invocations to the gods of love, asking that their powers intervene to harmonize or intensify the feelings between the couple. In some cases, the use of elements such as honey and flowers - symbols of sweetness and attraction - was a central part of these rituals, representing the desire for the relationship to flourish with gentleness and joy.

The influence of Isis in union rituals was particularly powerful. Known for her devotion to Osiris, Isis was seen as the goddess who preserved and strengthened the conjugal bond. The myth of Isis and Osiris, in which Isis searches for and resurrects the body of her dead husband, symbolizes the eternity of love and its ability to overcome even death. This myth served as an example for Egyptian couples, who saw in Isis a model of loyalty, perseverance, and unconditional love. In times of marital difficulty, the couple could make offerings to Isis, asking her to intercede and help restore harmony.

Another common practice in love rituals was the use of talismans. The "knot of Isis," one of the most powerful amulets of protection and union, was often given to couples at the beginning of their life together. This amulet, with its intertwined loop design, represented the unbreakable union between two souls and their divine connection. The knot of Isis was worn by couples as a symbol of protection against fights and misunderstandings, ensuring that negative energies did not disturb the serenity of the relationship.

Celebrations in honor of love also involved moments of celebration and joy, where music and dance played a central role. The celebrations held in the temples of Hathor were especially lively, with the priestesses singing songs dedicated to the goddess, accompanied by drums and stringed instruments. The sacred dances, often performed around statues or symbols of Hathor, represented the energy of love flowing freely, creating an atmosphere of harmony and fulfillment.

These rituals of love and union were, for the Egyptians, more than just traditions. They reflected the deep belief that love, when blessed by the gods, became a lasting force, capable of overcoming challenges and bringing eternal happiness. Through these spiritual practices, couples sought not only to live in harmony on earth but to ensure that their love transcended time, continuing even in the realm of the gods, where their souls would be eternally united.

Throughout their lives, couples in ancient Egypt faced the natural challenges of any human relationship. However, contrary to what it might seem, moments of disharmony were seen as an opportunity to strengthen ties, renewing love under divine protection. When conflicts or misunderstandings arose, reconciliation rituals assumed a vital role in restoring marital harmony.

At these times, Egyptians resorted to spells, amulets, and prayers, seeking the help of the gods to bring peace back to the home.

Hathor and Isis, once again, were the main deities invoked in reconciliation rituals. Hathor, with her loving and joyful nature, was called upon to dispel the shadows that enveloped the relationship, bringing back the light of understanding. In the temple of Dendera, dedicated to Hathor, priests performed ceremonies on behalf of couples seeking to renew their bonds. Small statues of the goddess, adorned with flowers and jewels, were offered as a symbol of beauty and harmony, with the intention that the couple could remember the feelings that originally united them.

When conflicts became more serious, Isis was invoked as the great protector of conjugal bonds. Just as she had restored Osiris after his death, it was believed that she could also restore peace and love between couples in times of crisis. In the temples, priestesses of Isis chanted songs of reconciliation, asking the goddess to calm hearts and heal emotional wounds. Small purification rituals were also performed, where couples drank sacred water that had been consecrated on the altar of Isis, believing that this water could cleanse the tensions that had arisen between them.

Reconciliation amulets played an essential role in these rituals. One of the most powerful was the "knot of Isis," already present in many marriages, but used in a special way during rites of restoration of harmony. The knot represented the sacred bond between spouses and, when consecrated again by the priests, functioned as a renewal of the commitment to union. This amulet was placed in the home or worn directly by couples, reinforcing their promise to overcome any challenge together, with the support of the deities.

In addition to direct interventions in temples, reconciliation rituals could be performed within the homes themselves. The couple, in times of crisis, could light an oil lamp on the home altar dedicated to Hathor or Isis, reciting prayers that asked for the restoration of love and harmony. This practice, in addition to being symbolic, served as a moment of joint reflection, where the spouses could reconnect with their spirituality and with each other, in search of a deeper and mutual understanding. The flame of the lamp represented the light of wisdom and love, which should be kept burning to guide the relationship along peaceful paths.

Reconciliation rituals often included the use of perfumes and sacred oils, especially those consecrated in the name of Hathor, who, as the goddess of beauty and sensuality, brought back the sweetness lost in the relationship. These oils were used to anoint the couple, in a symbolic gesture of physical and spiritual renewal, restoring desire and affection that may have been weakened by the tensions of daily life. The simple act of anointing the body with these oils transformed into an intimate and healing ritual, where physical contact was full of spiritual meaning.

Reconciliation enchantments were also part of the rituals. These spells were written on papyri or engraved on small clay tablets, which were left on the altars of the gods or buried near the couple's home. The sacred words, carefully chosen, invoked the help of the deities of love to strengthen the bond between the couple, warding off invisible forces that could be causing disagreements. Many of these enchantments were recited by the spouses themselves during the night, in moments of privacy, to ensure that feelings of love would flourish again.

In addition to reconciliation rituals, there were also annual celebrations that served to strengthen the bonds of union, even in times of peace. During festivals dedicated to Hathor and Isis, couples participated in processions and banquets that celebrated love and togetherness. At these events, joy and festivity played a central role. Musicians and dancers enlivened the streets and temples, while offerings of fruits, breads, and flowers were given to the priests to be consecrated. Laughter, dancing, and singing were ways to exalt loving union and reaffirm shared happiness.

Reconciliation was not just a matter of resolving conflicts, but of celebrating the renewal of love. Many couples, after performing the rituals of healing and union, made a point of renewing their spiritual vows in later offerings, bringing gifts to the gods again as a way of thanking them for their intervention. Thus, the cycle of love and harmony was perpetuated, reinforced by the belief that by maintaining a relationship protected by divine forces, love bonds would become unbreakable.

In Egyptian homes, the constant presence of amulets and statues of deities such as Hathor, Isis, and Bes, the protective god of families, reminded couples that their love was not just an earthly connection, but a part of the cosmic balance. Each gesture of affection, each word of reconciliation, was a reaffirmation of this sacred link, always renewed by the rituals that ensured that the union between mortals was blessed by the gods. In this way, the Egyptians believed that, even in the midst of adversity, love, protected and nurtured by rituals, was an eternal force that would transcend time and space, guiding couples to a life in harmony both on earth and in the afterlife.

Chapter 9
Rituals of Justice and Balance

At the center of the Egyptians' spiritual life hovered a concept that permeated both daily life and the deepest mysteries of the afterlife: Ma'at. Represented as a winged goddess, carrying the feather of truth on her head, Ma'at symbolized cosmic order, truth, and justice. It was she who balanced the forces of chaos, establishing a harmony that connected the world of the gods and that of mortals. For the Egyptians, living in accordance with Ma'at was essential not only to ensure a prosperous life on earth but also to ensure favorable judgment after death.

The life of an Egyptian was, therefore, a constant search for this balance. Rituals of justice and balance were fundamental, as they ensured that the individual, the family, and society itself remained in harmony with cosmic forces. The goddess Ma'at was invoked in situations of conflict, injustice, or disorder, and her role went far beyond the simple concept of justice as it is understood today. She represented the alignment of the soul with the universe, a path of righteousness that should be followed in all actions of life.

Rituals related to justice and balance began with the invocation of Ma'at in temples and home altars.

Before the statue of the goddess, simple offerings, such as bread, flowers, and small pieces of gold, were placed to ask for her intervention in judicial matters or in moments of personal imbalance. This act of offering was accompanied by prayers that sought to harmonize the heart and mind of the supplicant, allowing him to see clearly the truths that the goddess represented. Many of these rituals were performed in the dead of night, where the light of a sacred lamp symbolized the flame of truth, always shining in the heart of one who lives under the gaze of Ma'at.

In times of legal disputes, the Egyptians believed that Ma'at manifested herself directly in the decisions of judges and in the oracles consulted. The judgment of an important matter did not take place without a priest first performing purification and invocation rituals. These rituals involved sacred baths and the recitation of enchantments that ensured that the truth would be revealed. It was not uncommon for ostrich feathers - one of the most important symbols of Ma'at - to be used during the trial, either as protective amulets or as visible symbols of commitment to the truth.

In many of these rituals, ostrich feathers were consecrated with sacred oils and then given to judges or parties involved in a dispute. The feather symbolized the lightness that truth should have in everyone's heart, indicating that, to live in harmony with Ma'at, the individual should have a pure heart, free from falsehoods and deceit. The use of amulets, such as the ankh (symbol of life) or the ansate cross, was also common in these trials, representing the balanced and just life that one sought to maintain in accordance with the cosmic order.

Balance was not a concept limited to trials and legal matters. In Ma'at rituals, balance also concerned harmony within the community itself. The annual festivals and celebrations dedicated to the goddess were times when society came together to renew its bonds and ensure that all aspects of life - from family life to agricultural activities - were aligned with the order of the universe. On these occasions, sacred dances and music were dedicated to Ma'at, in processions that symbolized the harmonious flow of life. Each step of the dance was a reflection of the harmony between heaven and earth, between heart and mind.

Community rituals, such as the celebration of the harvest or annual festivals in honor of the protector gods, were also governed by Ma'at. Before the start of major celebrations, it was common for priests to purify altars and consecrate the ground with incense and holy water, ensuring that the event was blessed with balance and harmony. The idea was that by aligning the community with the principles of Ma'at, positive energies would flow freely, warding off chaos and any influence that could unbalance the natural cycle of life.

These rituals also involved oracles, which were consulted in times of crisis or uncertainty. The belief that Ma'at could be invoked to bring clarity and truth was so strong that many oracles were considered the direct voice of the goddess. The priest or priestess, in a trance, answered the questions of the community, always seeking to align the answers with the principles of justice and balance represented by the goddess. In many of these cases, the oracle's response determined the course of decisions, from judgments to choices about crops and construction.

Life in ancient Egypt was intrinsically linked to these notions of justice and balance. Each individual was responsible for keeping their heart and actions in accordance with Ma'at, and the rituals served as a constant reminder of this responsibility. Not only the individual, but society itself and the government should be balanced under the watchful eye of the goddess. The pharaohs, considered the divine representatives on earth, were the main guardians of Ma'at. Before major political or military decisions, the pharaoh consulted the priests of Ma'at to ensure that their actions were in accordance with the cosmic order, and that they did not bring imbalance or chaos to the kingdom.

Maintaining this balance was no simple task, and purification rituals played a crucial role in this process. Before any major decision or important event, both the pharaoh and the priests underwent purification rituals, where the sacred water of the Nile and perfumed oils were used to cleanse any spiritual impurity. Only after these practices could the ritual in the name of Ma'at begin, ensuring that the hearts and minds of all involved were attuned to the truth and justice that she represented.

The Egyptians believed that by living according to Ma'at, both in daily life and in the larger spheres of politics and religion, they ensured the continuous flow of harmony in the universe. More than a simple moral code, Ma'at was the very fabric of existence, and the rituals that invoked her power were seen as a necessary alignment with the forces that governed both the visible and the invisible.

At the heart of Egyptian justice rituals, the balance between cosmic forces and earthly life was something that extended to all spheres of society. Each day, the universal harmony, maintained by the goddess Ma'at, needed to be reaffirmed not only by individual acts, but also by collective ceremonies that ensured the constant flow of this invisible force that sustained the cosmos. If the balance were broken, the forces of chaos, known as Isfet, could infiltrate and disrupt both spiritual life and social order.

Egyptian communities often resorted to spiritual mediation rituals to resolve disputes and restore order. When conflicts arose, the role of the priest or priestess of Ma'at was crucial, as they acted as intermediaries between the world of men and the divine order. These mediators not only applied the code of laws of the land, but also performed ceremonies to align the spirit of those involved with the universal principles of truth and justice. Before any decision was made, offerings were made to the goddess so that her wisdom would guide the judgments.

The temple became a sacred court, where every word and gesture reverberated with the weight of cosmic balance. In these rituals, the use of incense and sacred music created an atmosphere of purity, as if each sound and fragrance were part of an invocation to Ma'at herself. The presence of ostrich feathers, associated with the lightness of truth, was common, reminding everyone that the weight of truth should be balanced with compassion and justice.

In ritualistic trials, it was not uncommon for the priest or priestess to use sacred objects, such as the "Eye of Horus," to intensify spiritual vision and ensure that decisions were made without any deviation from the path of truth. The "Eye of Horus," a symbol of divine vigilance, not only protected trials from evil influences, but also ensured that the answers given by the oracle were in perfect harmony with Ma'at. Trials, thus, were not just legal events, but also spiritual moments where the cosmos itself was consulted.

Disputes within communities, often centered on land, crops, or inheritance issues, were seen as reflections of imbalance between individuals. The presence of a priest who embodied the wisdom of Ma'at became essential to pacify these tensions. To restore harmony, reconciliation rituals were conducted at the end of each trial, where participants drank sacred water and shared blessed bread, symbolizing the restoration of peace and the return to cosmic order. This ritualized sharing was not just a symbolic act, but a spiritual reconnection, a renewal of the ties that bound society together.

The decisions of the trials were recorded on papyri, as a physical reminder that the truth had been reached. These documents were often kept in temples, in sacred archives, protected by the power of Ma'at. For the Egyptians, writing was a divine gift, and recording the outcome of a dispute in the name of justice was a way of sealing the agreement with the goddess herself, ensuring that the balance was not broken again. In addition, these documents served as a warning that deviation from the truth or a return to chaos would have serious consequences.

Among the most powerful rituals related to cosmic balance was the "renewal feast," where the community gathered in celebrations dedicated to Ma'at and other gods, such as Amun-Ra, who personified the power of the sun and divine order. At these festivals, offerings were taken to temples, and ritual dances, often performed by priestesses of Ma'at, imitated the movements of the universe, symbolizing the continuous return of harmony after each cycle of imbalance. These festivals were essential to the community, as they ensured that, despite conflicts and challenges, balance would always prevail.

A crucial aspect of Egyptian justice rituals was the role of oracles. Consulted in sacred temples, oracles were seen as the voice of the gods, especially Ma'at, who answered human questions through signs and symbols. Consulting an oracle began with purification rituals, where the supplicant underwent sacred baths and wore clean clothes before entering the sacred precinct. The priests then invoked Ma'at, asking the goddess to bring clarity to the question that would be presented.

The process of interpreting oracles was shrouded in mystery. The answers often came in the form of visions or symbols that needed to be deciphered by trained priests. In some cases, the oracle used sunlight or the position of the stars to indicate the answer, showing that the balance of earth and sky was always interconnected. The outcome of this consultation was not only an answer to earthly questions but a reaffirmation that the cosmos was in tune with human needs, always ready to intervene when chaos threatened.

The priests, when communicating what the oracle revealed, made a point of relating the answers to the principles of Ma'at. If an individual or community was out of balance, the oracle's answer would be clear: a return to truth and order was necessary to avoid major calamities. Often, these rituals of consulting the oracle were followed by special offerings, which included everything from small statues of the goddess to sacred foods, symbolizing the restoration of peace and harmony.

One of the most feared, but also most respected, rituals was the judgment of a corrupted heart. When someone was accused of a serious crime that defied the principles of Ma'at, the trial included the rite of weighing the heart, symbolized in ceremonies performed in special temples. The heart of the accused, represented in amulets or symbolic figures, was placed on a scale before the statue of Ma'at, where its purity would be tested. If the heart was lighter than or equal to the feather of Ma'at, this indicated that the individual had lived in harmony with justice. However, if the heart was heavy, the individual would face spiritual consequences, often believing that their soul would be devoured by Ammit, the ferocious creature that personified divine punishment.

These trials, although rare, were dramatic examples of the power of Egyptian rituals to maintain order and balance. The fear of Isfet, chaos, was ever-present, and the constant practice of justice rituals was seen as a way to keep the balance of the universe intact. More than a simple matter of legality, these rituals were understood as a collective effort to maintain harmony between the spiritual and material worlds.

The balance of Ma'at was, ultimately, the pillar on which all of Egyptian society rested. Her invisible presence guided every action, decision, and rite. Staying aligned with this balance meant not only prosperity in earthly life, but also the guarantee of a safe passage through the afterlife, where the spirit would continue to live in harmony with the gods, sustained by eternal truth and justice.

Chapter 10
Rituals of Wisdom and Knowledge

In the hushed shadows of Egyptian temples, where sunlight barely grazed the stones, scribes and initiates sought the foundation of all knowledge: the wisdom of the gods. It was Thoth, the god of writing, wisdom, and magic, who guided these dedicated souls, leading them through the deepest mysteries of the cosmos. He who had created words and recorded the laws was the silent master who ruled the realm of the intellect.

In Egypt, acquiring wisdom was not merely a quest for practical knowledge; it was a spiritual journey. It was believed that understanding the laws of the universe was also understanding the gods, and therefore, knowledge was the key to connecting with the divine. From an early age, those destined for writing and study were initiated into rituals that connected them directly to Thoth. Before touching the first pen or drawing the first hieroglyph, a young scribe underwent a purification ritual symbolizing the beginning of their journey on the path of knowledge.

Temples dedicated to Thoth, especially those in Hermopolis, were repositories of knowledge, but also sacred places of meditation and study. The libraries of these temples, many hidden in deep chambers and accessible only to initiates, were guardians of scrolls containing ancestral secrets, many of which were believed to be dictated by Thoth himself. The mere approach to these sacred texts required preparatory rituals, for handling sacred words without due reverence and purity could bring imbalance to both the individual and the cosmos.

In daily rituals, scribes and priests invoked Thoth through prayers and sacred chants. The whispered words were charged with power, each syllable carefully chosen to honor the god. In the stillness of the mornings, as the sun began to rise above the horizon, the scribes lit oil lamps and recited texts written on ancient scrolls. These recitations, often passed down through generations, were seen as a form of direct communion with Thoth, a way to open the mind to the hidden wisdom that permeated the universe.

The relationship between the scribes and Thoth was one of deep devotion. On clear nights, under the moonlight, when silence dominated the desert, many would retreat to meditate on the mysteries of knowledge. The moon, associated with Thoth for its connection to the cycle of time and hidden secrets, was seen as a symbol of enlightenment, bringing to light truths hidden in the darkness. The scribes believed that in these moments of stillness and contemplation, Thoth himself guided them on their journey of understanding, revealing insights and visions.

In addition to scribes, priests who dedicated themselves to the study of esoteric wisdom also performed rituals to enhance their connection with the divine. Many of these practices involved the writing and reading of sacred texts, considered portals to transcendental knowledge. The act of writing was itself a ritual, where each symbol, each hieroglyph, was drawn with precision and intention. The scribe or priest became a channel between the visible and invisible worlds, and the pen, dipped in ink, transformed into an instrument of power, capturing the wisdom of the gods in each line.

Esoteric learning in Egypt was not limited to the study of scriptures. Initiates were trained in the art of observation, both of the natural world and the signs that came from the heavens. The movement of the stars and planets was interpreted as a divine language, and those who mastered this knowledge were able to predict events and understand the messages of the gods. Thoth, as god of time and measure, taught his followers to read these signs accurately, connecting celestial knowledge to the terrestrial. Each star, each constellation, was seen as a reflection of the divine order, and understanding these patterns was essential to achieving true wisdom.

The rituals of wisdom, however, were not just solitary. Many scribes and priests gathered in collective ceremonies where learning was shared and exalted. In these ceremonies, conducted in the temples of Thoth, the most experienced taught the younger ones the secrets they had learned throughout their lives. The learning process was considered sacred, and each new lesson was accompanied by rituals of thanksgiving to the god. Small offerings, such as figs, honey, and incense, were burned before the statues of Thoth, in gratitude for the divine generosity in granting humans the gift of writing and knowledge.

The use of amulets also played an important role in these rituals. One of the most powerful was the symbol of the "Ibis," the bird associated with Thoth, which was worn as a talisman of protection and wisdom. The amulets, consecrated in temples and blessed by priests, were carried by scribes and scholars to ensure that their minds remained open to enlightenment and their hands were guided by divinity. Wearing the Ibis amulet was a constant reminder that the path of wisdom was a divine gift that demanded devotion and respect.

The quest for wisdom was also deeply connected to magic. The sacred texts contained enchantments and magic formulas, which, when recited correctly, could influence both the physical and spiritual worlds. The priests of Thoth were both scribes and magicians, guardians of knowledge that transcended the barriers of everyday reality. Learning rituals often involved memorizing these enchantments, and initiates were trained to recite the sacred words with the exact intonation and rhythm, believing that by doing so, they could directly access divine power.

Those who followed the path of Thoth sought not only knowledge for its own sake but also a deeper understanding of life and death, time and eternity. Each written word, each text read, was a new piece in the cosmic puzzle they sought to unravel. For the ancient Egyptians, wisdom was not an end, but a means of connecting with the divine, of transcending the limitations of the material world and touching the eternal truth that governed the universe. Thoth, the great scribe of the gods, guided his followers on this path of mystery and revelation, where knowledge became light, and light, understanding.

In the depths of the temples, where sacred silence enveloped the ancient stones and the air carried the scent of incense, priests and initiates gathered in search of higher knowledge. For those who followed the mysteries of Thoth, knowledge was never static. Each new discovery, each deciphered symbol, represented a bridge to invisible realms where the spirit of divine wisdom awaited those who were prepared to receive it. The path of learning, however, required more than just reading or observation; it was deeply spiritual and often involved rituals of personal transformation.

The rituals of esoteric learning were not limited to a simple study of texts. In the most sacred temples, those seeking true enlightenment were introduced to ceremonies where the recitation of ancient sacred texts was accompanied by meditations and visualizations. The initiates, in their white robes, sat in circles around a central flame, whose flames flickered to the rhythm of silent prayers. Each word, each syllable, was charged with the power of the universe, and as the voices echoed, the environment seemed to merge with the cosmos, creating a state of heightened consciousness where the boundaries between human and divine disappeared.

Within these rituals, the repetition of sacred texts, known as heka (words of power), was central. These words were not mere enchantments, but magic formulas that, when recited with the correct intonation and a pure heart, opened doors to hidden dimensions. The priests of Thoth believed that by repeating these formulas daily, the initiate not only expanded their intellect but also purified their soul, becoming worthy of receiving wisdom directly from the gods. In the deepest moments of these rituals, many believed they felt the presence of Thoth, the ibis-headed god, whose eyes watched, approving or challenging each step of the spiritual journey.

Inside the sacred libraries, initiates did not have full access to the most secret texts immediately. Knowledge rituals were divided into levels, and only the most advanced could handle the scrolls containing the most powerful formulas. These scrolls, written in intricate hieroglyphs, were attributed secrets of the universe: from the cycle of stars to the magic of spiritual transformation. The process of deciphering these formulas was itself a rite of passage. With each symbol that was revealed, the initiate felt closer to Thoth, as if, through ink and papyrus, the god himself was whispering to them the secrets of creation.

Meditation was another central practice in these rituals of seeking wisdom. Along the tranquil banks of the Nile, initiates sat in silence, contemplating the movement of the waters. For the ancient Egyptians, the Nile was not just a river, but a tangible manifestation of the cosmic flow. Observing its movement was, for the wise, like observing the course of life itself. Sitting in deep meditation, the disciples learned to synchronize their thoughts and breaths with the natural rhythm of the universe. Silence was essential because in it, they believed, the answers to the deepest mysteries could be heard.

Among the esoteric practices, there was also the use of dreams as a means of receiving divine knowledge. In the temples dedicated to Thoth, there were special chambers where initiates spent the night, in a state of sleep induced by chants and specific aromas, in the hope that their minds, free from the distractions of the physical world, could receive messages and visions directly from the gods. These dreams, carefully interpreted by the priests the next morning, were seen as direct guidance, indicating the right path to follow, revealing hidden secrets, or warning of imminent dangers.

Among the practices of esoteric learning, there was also a deep connection between wisdom and spiritual power. The priests of Thoth were not only scholars; they were also magicians, capable of manipulating invisible forces through the combination of knowledge and ritual practice. Learning magic formulas involved both oral repetition and ritualistic practice. The initiates trained incessantly to master the enchantments that, when used correctly, could transform the reality around them. These magic formulas were seen as the ultimate expression of wisdom, since they translated divine knowledge into practical action in the material world.

In the most advanced practices, initiates were introduced to the mysteries of creation, where they learned about the power of words in the formation of the universe. For the followers of Thoth, the word had the power to create and destroy. Thus, learning rituals included long sessions of writing and recitation, where the disciple practiced the art of "speaking the world." Each carefully drawn hieroglyph carried a subtle energy that, when activated by the voice, manifested itself on the physical plane. Writing, therefore, was not just a means of recording knowledge, but a tool for shaping reality itself.

Among the deepest secrets taught in the temples of Thoth was the art of "weighing words." This concept, although related to the judgment of the soul, also applied to learning. Just as the heart was weighed against the feather of Ma'at in the underworld court, the words of a scribe or priest were measured by the truth they carried. Learning rituals, therefore, emphasized not only intellectual mastery, but also purity of intention and harmony with cosmic laws. Only those who mastered this balance could progress to the highest levels of esoteric knowledge.

At the conclusion of learning rituals, initiates often received sacred amulets, symbols of Thoth's protection and the wisdom acquired. These amulets, such as the "Eye of Horus" or the "Ankh," were consecrated in special ceremonies, where priests invoked the presence of the god to bless and protect those who now carried the burden of divine knowledge. The amulet, hung on the chest or kept in a sacred place, served as a constant reminder of the responsibility that accompanied esoteric learning.

Thus, the rituals of wisdom and knowledge in Ancient Egypt were not just ways of acquiring practical or theoretical knowledge. They were gateways to understanding realities far beyond what human eyes could see. The initiates, throughout their journey, sought not only an understanding of the material world, but also a deeper connection with the divine. They knew that by deciphering each text, uttering each enchantment, and observing each star, they were participating in something much greater—a cosmic dance that echoed from the creation of the universe. And Thoth, the great scribe of the gods, was the silent guide who led them through these paths of mystery and enlightenment.

Chapter 11
Rituals of Purification and Spiritual Cleansing

As the sun slowly rose over the banks of the Nile, Egypt awoke enveloped in an atmosphere of reverence. For the ancient Egyptians, life was a perpetual cycle of renewal, and purity, both of body and spirit, was essential to maintain this sacred connection with the gods. Each dawn represented a new chance for purification, to start anew, cleansed, both in the physical and spiritual worlds. And it was through the rituals of purification that this cycle of cleansing and spiritual renewal manifested itself.

Water, especially that of the Nile River, was the main symbol of purification. This river, which the Egyptians considered a gift from the gods, carried within it the power to cleanse, heal, and renew. In many purification rituals, priests bathed in its waters, believing that upon emerging, their souls and bodies would be free from all accumulated impurity. Ritual bathing was not a practice limited to priests; ordinary people also participated in rituals at festivals or before important events, immersing themselves in the Nile or in special basins in temples, which contained consecrated waters.

The practice of ritual bathing symbolized much more than simple physical cleansing. For the Egyptians, spiritual impurity could accumulate from negative thoughts, disordered emotions, or actions that defied the cosmic order. Thus, each immersion in the sacred waters was a way to restore inner balance, reconnecting with divine forces and ensuring that the blessings of the gods flowed freely. In more solemn ceremonies, the water was mixed with special herbs and oils, infusing it with even more intense healing powers.

In addition to water, the use of incense was a fundamental practice in purification rituals. The aroma of incense, rising in the air, carried with it spiritual impurities and dissolved them in the wind, like a fragrant offering to the gods. The herbs and resins used were carefully selected, each chosen for its specific spiritual properties. Frankincense incense, for example, was known for its ability to ward off negative energies, while myrrh, with its sweet and earthy scent, brought calm and serenity to the hearts of those participating in the rituals.

In the inner chambers of the temples, priests lit incense before the statues of the gods, while chanting ancient chants that invoked the presence of the protecting deities. The dense perfume filled the air, creating an atmosphere of sanctity and peace. In many ceremonies, incense smoke was used to "wash" sacred objects, as well as the bodies of priests and participants, drawing invisible lines of protection around them. Divine figures, such as those of Osiris and Isis, received this smoke as an offering, symbolizing that all impure energy was being transmuted into harmony.

On a personal level, amulets also played an important role in spiritual protection and purification. These small sacred objects, often made of precious stones or metals, were worn on the body or kept in homes to ward off evil influences. Before being used, however, the amulets underwent a purification ritual, where they were bathed in holy water and passed through incense smoke. This process "activated" them, imbuing them with the divine power to ward off evil and attract good energies. The "Eye of Horus," one of the most popular amulets, was widely used as a shield against negative energies, in addition to bringing spiritual clarity.

In times of great crisis or danger, such as illness or omens of bad luck, purification became an even greater priority. The Egyptians believed that these moments were manifestations of spiritual imbalance, and purification rituals, often performed en masse, became essential to restore harmony. On these occasions, large processions took place through the streets and banks of the Nile, where the community, together, participated in collective purification ceremonies. The smoke of incense filled the air, and the chants reverberated through the waters of the river, echoing on the banks and invoking the protection of the gods.

Priests, as guardians of the cosmic order, had a central role in these ceremonies. Before performing any ritual, they themselves underwent extensive purification processes. From dawn, they repeatedly bathed in holy water, lit incense, and used scented oils that purified not only their bodies but also their minds and hearts. At the end of this process, they were ready to serve as intermediaries between the world of mortals and that of the gods, ensuring that sacred energies flowed without obstruction.

The use of sacred instruments in rituals was also part of this purification process. Objects such as gold and silver basins, ritual wands, and bells were carefully cleaned and consecrated before being used in ceremonies. These instruments were considered extensions of divine power, and their purity was essential to ensure the effectiveness of the rituals. When a priest poured holy water from one of these basins, for example, it was believed that the very essence of Osiris or Isis flowed along, blessing and purifying all who were present.

Purification was not just physical or spiritual, but also emotional. The rituals offered an opportunity for participants to free themselves from the anxieties, fears, and sorrows that haunted them. By chanting or reciting prayers to the gods, negative emotions were gradually released, leaving room for serenity and inner balance. These rituals were seen as a form of healing, for both body and soul, restoring the natural state of harmony that the Egyptians believed to be the divine ideal.

These purification practices were particularly important at times of transition, such as before major religious celebrations or after a period of mourning. The end of one cycle and the beginning of another were critical moments when balance needed to be restored. Before participating in festivals dedicated to the gods, such as the "Festival of the Beauty of Isis," for example, people performed purification rituals to ensure that they were spiritually ready to receive the blessings of the goddess.

With nightfall, purification continued, but now with a different focus: cleansing the environment. Homes were swept, sacred spaces tidied, and incense burned at doors and windows to protect against evil spirits and unwanted influences. Talismans were placed at the entrances of houses, symbolizing that the protection of the gods was present. The air was charged with a renewed energy, and Egyptian homes became places of peace, where the gods were welcome and negative energies had no room to enter.

These purification rituals, both individual and communal, ensured that the constant flow of life and death, chaos and order, was always in balance. And as the cycle of the day continued, the Egyptians knew that with each sunrise, a new chance for renewal awaited them, and that through rituals, they would remain connected to the eternal harmony of the universe.

In the depths of the Egyptian temples, where silence reverberated among the stone columns and ancient hieroglyphs seemed to come to life in the flickering torchlight, the most complex purification rituals took place. These rites, reserved for special occasions or major celebrations, were events that transcended the simple cleansing of the body or soul. It was a spiritual refinement, a true preparation for those moments when the connection with the divine needed to be absolute, without any interference from the physical world or the impurities of everyday life.

Before any major religious festival, the priests dedicated themselves to a rigorous purification process that could last for days. These preparations were necessary for them to be completely cleansed and ready to conduct the rituals that would ensure the balance between the world of the gods and that of men. The ceremonies demanded total concentration and a purity that went beyond appearance, delving into the depths of the soul. In these moments, spiritual cleansing rituals involved repeated baths in the sacred waters of the Nile, accompanied by continuous prayers invoking the protection and power of gods like Osiris and Isis.

Water, always central to any purification rite, gained even more importance during these ceremonies. The basins of holy water, used to wash not only the bodies of the priests, but also the objects of worship, were adorned with symbols of protection, such as the Ankh and the Eye of Horus. By pouring water over themselves or over the altars, the priests believed they were participating in an eternal cycle of renewal, where the forces of chaos were washed away, and the world was recreated in harmony.

Sacred instruments, such as golden basins or ritual wands, also underwent careful purification. Before each festival, these objects were anointed with aromatic oils and perfumed with incense, while chants reverberated through the sacred chambers. These practices not only physically cleansed the objects, but charged them with spiritual energy, making them worthy of touching the sacred and serving as intermediaries between the human and divine worlds. Many believed that these instruments, when properly purified, carried the very power of the gods, becoming vehicles of spiritual power.

However, it was not only within the temples that these purification rituals took place. Before major festivals, the cities along the Nile also underwent a symbolic cleansing process. Streets were swept, public spaces purified with incense smoke, and community altars adorned with fresh flowers and offerings. This collective purification reflected the belief that not only the priests, but all the people needed to be spiritually cleansed to receive the blessings of the gods.

The grandeur of these purification rituals reached its climax at the annual festivals, such as the Festival of the Arrival of Isis. During these events, Egypt itself seemed to breathe renewed purity. Before the start of the celebrations, the priestesses of Isis conducted sacred cleansing rites, where participants were anointed with perfumed oils and given protective amulets. The use of herbs like myrrh and sandalwood was common, their fragrances filling the air and uplifting the spirits of those seeking inner renewal. These oils, mixed with Nile water, were applied to the temples, hands, and feet of the faithful, symbolizing entry into a state of absolute purity.

The heart of the Egyptian festivals, however, was the grand procession in which the statue of the god or goddess was carried by priests in sacred boats, floating on the waters of the Nile. Before this procession, the statue underwent complex purification rituals, where it was bathed in consecrated water, dressed in fine fabrics, and adorned with sacred jewels. These rituals symbolized the rebirth of the god or goddess themselves, a moment of cosmic purification, where chaos was momentarily subdued, and the divine order reaffirmed.

During these moments, the Nile became more than a river; it was the vein of divine purification, connecting Egypt to the spiritual world. The reflection of the water, rippling under the sun, seemed to carry with it the prayers of all those seeking purification and renewal. The offerings, thrown into the river, floated gently on the currents, carrying with them the hopes, fears, and prayers of the faithful. Each offering, whether a small clay sculpture or a fragrant flower, represented a desire for purification, a plea for the sacred waters of the Nile to wash away all impurities.

Music, always present in Egyptian rituals, played a crucial role in these moments. The sound of harps and flutes echoed along the banks of the Nile, creating a soft melody that accompanied the rhythm of the waters. The chants of the priestesses, melodic and hypnotic, invoked the forces of nature, asking that the cycle of purification be complete. Music, thus, was transformed into a channel for the sacred, a bridge between the earthly and spiritual worlds, through which total purification could be achieved.

Another powerful element in purification rituals was the use of salt. Considered a symbol of preservation and purity, salt was often scattered on altars and sacred circles, drawing barriers that prevented the entry of evil or disorderly forces. In the most important ceremonies, salt was mixed with holy water, creating a solution that was used to sprinkle participants, sacred objects, and temples. It was believed that this mixture created an invisible barrier, protecting those participating in the ritual and warding off any negative influences.

In temples dedicated to gods like Osiris and Isis, the purification ritual was often accompanied by silent prayers, where each priest connected with the divine individually. These moments of introspection were fundamental for purification to be complete. The priests believed that by cleansing their minds of impure thoughts and focusing solely on the sacred, they became channels of light through which the will of the gods could manifest.

The most intense purifications occurred before important transitional events, such as initiation rituals or passage into new life cycles. At these times, initiates went through various stages of purification, which included fasting, ritual baths, and intense prayers. These rituals aimed not only at physical cleansing, but also at the spiritual preparation necessary for the initiate to receive sacred knowledge or move on to a new stage of their spiritual journey. Each step of the process was guided by experienced priests, who carefully observed the signs of the initiate's inner purification before allowing them to advance to the final stages of the ritual.

Purification, therefore, was a practice that went far beyond the simple act of cleansing the body. It was a profound spiritual journey, a process of continuous renewal that allowed the Egyptians to remain in harmony with the cosmos and the gods. In temples, on the banks of the Nile, and in homes, the purification ritual was a constant, ensuring that the cycle of life, death, and rebirth continued to flow in perfect synchrony with divine forces. For the ancient Egyptians, purification was not just a means of achieving physical purity, but a way of aligning oneself with the eternal, a way of keeping the cosmic order ever-present in their lives.

Chapter 12
Protection Rituals against Curses and Evil Spirits

In the desolate lands of Egypt, where the desert shadows seemed to move with the breeze and the wind whispered ancient secrets, the Egyptians lived in a world permeated by unseen forces. For them, life's balance depended on constant vigilance against negative energies and evil influences that lurked in everyday life. Gods and spirits were everywhere, both to protect and to threaten. It was necessary to maintain protective rituals, designed to ward off curses and dark spirits, ensuring harmony in the physical and spiritual world.

Since earliest times, the fear of curses was part of Egyptian life. It was believed that a simple gesture or a malicious word could invoke negative forces, affecting a person's health, prosperity, and even their soul. To combat these evils, protection rituals became a common and essential practice. In homes, temples, and cultivated lands, the presence of amulets and offerings was a visible sign of the need for constant protection against these unseen dangers.

Among the most powerful and well-known protective artifacts was the Eye of Horus, also known as the Wedjat. This amulet, bearing the symbol of an eye, represented the watchful gaze of the god Horus and was widely used to ward off dangers that might approach, both on the physical and spiritual planes. Placed at the entrances of houses, hung around the neck or close to the body, the Eye of Horus was a powerful defense against evil spirits and curses cast by enemies or occult forces. It was believed that by wearing this symbol, the protective power of Horus was always present, watching and warding off any negative influence.

Protection rituals were performed both in times of great danger and on more mundane occasions. For example, when someone fell ill unexpectedly, the illness was often attributed to the presence of an evil spirit or a conjured curse. In this case, priests were called to perform rituals that purified the victim's body and spirit. The sick person was anointed with sacred oils and surrounded by incense, while magic formulas, known as heka, were recited to ward off evil. These incantations were passed down from generation to generation and considered so powerful that, if pronounced correctly, they could undo even the most serious curses.

Among the most feared and respected gods, Anubis, the guardian of the necropolis and the god associated with the protection of the dead, was often invoked in rituals of defense against evil spirits. In particular, Anubis was considered the protector of tombs, ensuring that the dead rested in peace and that their souls were not disturbed by negative forces. In many funerary rituals, offerings were made to Anubis, and his images were placed in tombs as a shield against any malicious invocation attempts. The presence of

Anubis was seen as a sign that the tomb was under divine protection, a sacred place where no evil spirit could penetrate.

In temples, the smoke from burning herbs and resins served as a spiritual barrier. Myrrh and frankincense, with their dense aromas, were burned incessantly, creating a cloud of protection that enveloped those who participated in the rituals. The smoke, seen as a vehicle of purification and defense, was directed towards the altars and sacred objects, cleansing them of any negative presence. In the most important ceremonies, priestesses dressed in white robes danced around the statues of the gods, lighting torches and waving branches of sacred plants, while reciting chants that invoked the gods to protect the temple and its visitors.

Another fundamental aspect of protection rituals against curses was the creation of magic circles. These circles, drawn on the ground with flour, sand, or salt, delimited a sacred area where negative forces could not penetrate. In more advanced rituals, these circles were drawn with sacred hieroglyphs, representing protective gods like Bastet, the lioness goddess, or Sekhmet, the warrior goddess. Within these circles, the priests conducted their ceremonies safely, certain that the barriers they had created were impenetrable to evil spirits. Any entity that dared to try to cross this invisible line would be immediately repelled by the powers of the gods invoked there.

The incantations used in these protection rituals were also carefully crafted. Some were recited aloud, so that the air itself would carry the sacred words and spread them as a protective barrier. Other incantations, however, were whispered, almost inaudible, intended only for the ears of the gods and protective spirits. The belief was that words, when pronounced with the correct intonation and intention, had the power to shape reality and alter the course of events, undoing curses and repelling any negative influence.

The use of figures and amulets also played a central role in these rituals. Statuettes of Bes, the dwarf god protector of the home and family, were placed in homes, especially in children's rooms and resting places. Bes, with his fierce and laughing face, was invoked to protect against nightmares and evil influences, warding off disturbing spirits that could cause harm during sleep. It was believed that his stern gaze kept demons at bay, ensuring the safety of all those under his care.

In agricultural lands, farmers performed similar rituals to protect their crops from pests and disasters. Invoking Horus and other protective gods, they traced sacred symbols in the fields, poured holy water into the furrows between the crops, and buried small amulets in the ground to ensure that the land remained fertile and free of curses. These rituals, performed seasonally, were fundamental to ensure not only physical survival but also the spiritual well-being of the community.

Protection from curses and evil spirits was, therefore, an essential practice that permeated all aspects of Egyptian life. From the humblest peasants to the powerful priests, all recognized that the unseen forces of chaos and destruction could manifest at any moment.

The rituals, carefully preserved and passed down through the centuries, were the first and last line of defense against these threats, ensuring that the cosmic order prevailed over chaos and that souls, both living and dead, remained safe in the protective hands of the gods.

On the banks of the Nile, the Egyptians always believed that the barrier between the visible and invisible world was tenuous. For them, the threat of curses and evil spirits constantly loomed, like a breeze that could suddenly change and bring destructive forces with it. Therefore, protection rituals were not just a spiritual practice, but a necessity that involved the use of powerful amulets and the recitation of ancient incantations that acted as shields against hidden dangers.

Among the most revered practices was the use of the Eye of Horus, a symbol that carried the essence of the protective vision of one of Egypt's most powerful gods. But besides it, another widely used amulet was the Scarab, a symbol of rebirth and protection against spiritual death. These small artifacts were buried with the dead so that their souls would be protected during the perilous journey through the world of the dead, but they were also used in life by those who feared curses cast by hidden enemies. The scarab, with its engravings, was also a way for the living to protect themselves against misfortune, evil, and interference from wandering spirits.

The relationship between the living and the dead, in many cases, was maintained through rituals aimed at appeasing restless souls or preventing those already buried from returning as vengeful spirits. In temples and tombs, it was common practice to inscribe magic formulas on the walls and doors of tombs, as a physical and spiritual barrier that prevented the entry of destructive forces. These formulas, called heka, were invocations to divinity and the universe itself to maintain balance between the two worlds.

The use of specific magic formulas during these rituals was an art mastered by priests, who possessed the knowledge of secret words. These formulas were carefully passed down through generations, and it was believed that incorrect pronunciation could nullify their power or even attract the evil they intended to ward off. The texts of the sarcophagi, for example, contained these invocations in abundance, ensuring that the deceased was protected against any attempt at disturbance by evil spirits or by those who wished to harm their journey in the afterlife.

The creation of amulets was a sacred craft. In temple workshops, artisans were tasked with forging pieces such as the Isis knot, which brought the protection of the great goddess and her ability to restore harmony. Amulets like these were often consecrated in special ceremonies, in which the priest chanted songs of protection while holding the object in his hand, imbuing it with sacred energy. An amulet was not just a piece of stone or metal — it was an extension of divine power, an intermediary between gods and humans, capable of warding off evil and ensuring the continued protection of the wearer.

On dark nights, when sandstorms swept the desert and the horizon merged with the sky, protection rituals reached their climax. It was at this time that Egyptian families gathered, lighting incense and candles before the statues of the gods. With unshakeable faith, they recited incantations learned from their elders, asking for the protection of Bastet, the lion-headed goddess whose sharp claws could ward off any spirit that tried to invade their homes.

Chapter 13
Rituals for Good Luck and Fortune

The Nile, with its ever-renewed waters, was not only the physical sustenance of the ancient Egyptian civilization but also a living symbol of luck and prosperity. For the Egyptians, each movement of its waters brought with it promises of abundant harvests, plentiful trade, and blessings for everyday life. However, to ensure that good luck never abandoned them, they resorted to a series of rituals dedicated to deities who controlled the whims of fate.

The figure of Hapi, the god of the Nile, was central to this scenario. He was not only a representation of the river but also the guardian of the abundance that its banks provided. In times of drought or uncontrolled floods, Hapi was called upon through offerings and chants. These rituals, often performed at the beginning of the harvest season, were fundamental to ensuring that the river brought the perfect balance between fertility and calm. Priests, along the banks, threw flowers and fruits into the waters, believing that these gifts would be well received by Hapi, who would reciprocate with abundance.

The amulet known as the Ankh, which symbolized life, was commonly used to attract luck. The

Egyptians carried it with them, believing that this simple object could ward off bad luck and open doors to unexpected opportunities. Similarly, the Eye of Horus was also a symbol used not only for protection but to bring prosperity. It was common to hang these amulets in places of commerce, at the entrances of houses, and in the fields, as a way of attracting good fortune.

In festivals dedicated to Hapi, abundance was celebrated in large public ceremonies. Men and women, adorned with flower crowns, danced to the sound of drums and flutes, invoking the energy of the river. Offerings were placed in baskets, containing bread, beer, and honey — the gods' preferred gifts. These communal rituals not only sought to ensure a good harvest but also protected the people against pests that, in difficult times, could destroy the fields.

In the bustling markets, merchants also resorted to personal rituals to ensure their sales were prosperous. Small altars dedicated to Ptah or Hathor, goddess of prosperity and joy, were common in the corners of stalls. Before starting the day, a brief prayer or an offering of incense was made, seeking to ensure that the day was full of luck and good transactions. For traders, these gestures were fundamental, as they believed that success depended both on work and divine blessing.

But luck, like the Nile, was seen as something that flowed and changed. There were times when the tide of life seemed to be against them, and at these times, the Egyptians resorted to more complex rituals, involving specific invocations and elaborate offerings. One such ritual, performed when bad luck seemed to plague a family or individual, included the use of holy water and newly consecrated amulets. Priests drew protective symbols in the sand, forming a circle around the affected person, while reciting words of power that were supposed to break the cycle of bad luck.

Collective feasts and rituals were a reminder that, in the view of the ancient Egyptians, luck was not just an individual factor, but something that involved the entire community. When the Nile rose in harmony, everyone prospered. When it lowered, everyone suffered. Thus, ensuring luck was a joint effort, and the gods needed to be constantly appeased, not just for individual interests but for the good of the whole society.

The full moon illuminated the vast desert, reflecting its brilliance on the tranquil waters of the Nile. It was the perfect time to perform the oldest and most powerful rituals, those that ensured good luck not only for individuals but for the entire community. The festivals that accompanied these rituals were occasions of celebration and reverence, where the blessings of the gods were requested in exchange for offerings that could ensure collective prosperity.

The festival of Opet, one of Egypt's greatest festivals, was one such special moment. During this festival, the gods Amun, Mut, and Khonsu were carried in procession across the Nile, from the city of Karnak to Luxor. Thousands of people gathered on the banks of the river, lighting candles and offering food. Prayers were chanted rhythmically, as if the very sound of voices could guide luck to the homes of the participants.

The belief was simple: by venerating the gods and strengthening the bonds between humans and the divine, luck would flow like the Nile, fertilizing both the fields and hearts.

Good fortune, however, was not just a matter of big festivals. Everyday life was also permeated by small rituals, discreet and silent, which ensured that bad luck was kept at bay. The use of talismans continued to be an essential practice, especially the amulet known as Bes, the dwarf god protector of homes and families. Bes was invoked to ward off evil spirits and ensure happiness within homes. Families kept small figures of this god at the entrances of their houses, believing that this would not only protect against misfortunes but also bring joy and prosperity.

Priests, holders of divine secrets, also played a crucial role in maintaining the community's good fortune. Many rituals required the presence of these divine intermediaries, who knew the correct words, precise gestures, and exact offerings to ensure that fortune never abandoned the people. Through chants and recitations of sacred texts, these priests performed ceremonies in temples especially dedicated to deities like Ra and Isis, seeking not only protection but the continuous flow of luck and abundance.

During harvest time, another good luck ritual often performed involved the consecration of seeds before planting. The seeds were dipped in holy water and placed on temporary altars, where priests recited prayers to ensure that, once planted, these seeds would produce a bountiful harvest. This ritual united agricultural magic with divine power, showing how, for the Egyptians, the prosperity of the land was intertwined with divine intervention.

Good luck spells also had unique importance. Magic texts were written on papyri and then buried under the foundations of houses or shops, to ensure that success and luck were literally built on these sacred foundations. In times of need, these inscriptions were read aloud, releasing the power of words to attract lost fortune.

In parallel with the incantations, there was also the power of gestures. Simple gestures, such as waving three times towards the rising sun or dipping your hands in the Nile at midnight, were seen as ways to connect directly with the forces of luck. Such gestures, performed at key moments of the day or year, ensured that the blessings of the gods were always available to those who dedicated themselves to keeping the tradition alive.

In times of crisis, when bad luck seemed to be more tangibly present, one of the most powerful rituals consisted of lighting seven oil lamps before the statue of Hathor. These small fires, fueled by perfumed oils, represented not only the light of hope but also the destruction of the darkness of adversity. As the lamps burned, devotees chanted prayers, asking Hathor to bring back luck and dispel the shadows that had settled in their lives.

These rituals, large and small, echoed through all layers of Egyptian society. From the humble farmer to the highest priest, everyone sought ways to ensure that luck remained by their side, flowing like the waters of the Nile, always constant, always renewed.

Chapter 14
Rituals of Rebirth and Transformation

For the Egyptians, death was not the end, but a necessary step towards renewal. The concept of rebirth permeated their worldview, and sacred stories, especially the myth of Osiris, revealed the mysteries of this transformation. It was he, the god who was murdered, dismembered, and resurrected by Isis, who served as a guide for all those who wished to cross the murky waters of death and emerge into a new, spiritual, and eternal life.

Rebirth rituals reflected this profound belief. They began in life, when initiates were prepared for their spiritual transitions. Each phase of their existence was a preparation for the great moment of transformation, where body and soul would separate, but with the purpose of reconfiguring themselves into something higher. Just as the grain that needs to die to bear fruit, the life of the individual needed to go through a process of symbolic "death" so that a new being could emerge, purified and strengthened.

In sacred temples, priests and initiates performed these rites in secret. Surrounded by symbols and relics of power, participants underwent intensive tests and purifications. Water, an essential element, represented both the natural cycle and the potential for spiritual renewal. Submerged in ritual baths, the initiates detached themselves from physical and spiritual impurities, while prayers and chants were intoned, evoking the presence of Osiris and the regenerative forces he represented.

During these ceremonies, amulets such as the "Isis knot" were used to seal the bonds between body and spirit, protecting the initiate during the transition. At the moment of greatest intensity of the ritual, the participant's eyes were blindfolded, and he symbolically crossed the abyss between life and death. This "ritual of blindness" was fundamental, as it represented the death of the physical senses and the activation of the spiritual senses, essential to guide the soul on the path of rebirth.

At the height of the ceremony, silence took over the temple. The priests, in a solemn position, awaited the sign that the transformation had taken place. The initiate, now reborn, emerged from the darkness of symbolic death into the light of a new existence, purified and in harmony with the cosmic forces. Rebirth was not just a spiritual concept, but a lived practice, where the individual prepared for his eternal destiny, becoming a living expression of the cycles of death and renewal that governed the universe.

The rebirth rituals, linked to the myth of Osiris, also served as a metaphor for community life. Just as the god of the dead was reborn to rule the underworld, kings and priests sought their own renewal through these rites, ensuring that the cycle of power and prosperity continued uninterrupted.

In the stillness of the temple, the wind of the ages moved the shadows of the columns, while the initiate, now in communion with ancestral forces, entered the final phase of rebirth. He was no longer the same. The transformed soul had crossed the thresholds that separated the visible from the invisible world, connecting to the ancient secrets kept by the priests. The cycle was about to be completed, and the last phase of this process was a profound consecration, where the reborn became a living bridge between the two worlds.

During these rituals, each step was meticulously calculated. Silence was not just an absence of sound, but a space where the spirit found its true voice. In an environment where soft incense lights danced in the air, the priests surrounded him, chanting sacred chants. The words, which seemed to echo from the stones of the temple, led the initiate's mind to higher planes of existence. Now, he was in communion with the entities that dwelt beyond the veil.

The transformation was not just symbolic. The Egyptians believed that, during the ritual, the physical body acquired a new power, a renewed vitality that connected it to the continuous flow of divine energies. The initiate saw himself as the river that crosses deserts, carrying with him the promise of life wherever it flowed. His gestures, his words, his thoughts were reflections of a new internal order, where death was no longer feared, but understood as an inevitable and necessary passage.

In one of the most intense moments, the high priest took in his hands the "tet", the sacred pillar of

Osiris, symbol of stability and continuity. This was raised in a ritual gesture, reflecting the eternal rebirth of the god who represented victory over chaos. The initiate, observing the movement, understood that his journey was intertwined with the destiny of the gods, and that his existence was part of something much greater, a cosmic tapestry woven with the threads of life, death, and renewal.

The final crossing was celebrated with the lighting of the ritual flames, a soft light, but full of meaning. Each flame lit represented the purification of an aspect of being, from the physical body to the highest spiritual planes. Around the altar, sacred objects - such as the eye of Horus and the Ankh symbol - radiated the energy of the gods, present there at that moment of transmutation. The initiate was ready to take his place in the cosmic cycle, from where he would be eternally reborn.

Chapter 15
Rituals of Conquest and Territorial Expansion

In the golden immensity of the desert, where the horizon seemed to merge with the bronze sky, the pharaoh prepared to lead his army towards new lands. The march of territorial expansion was not a mere military undertaking. In ancient Egypt, each conquest was a divine mission, and success depended on the favor of the gods. Therefore, before the first soldier raised his sword, sacred rituals were performed to ensure that celestial force accompanied every step of the warriors.

At the heart of the rituals was Montu, the god of war, whose imposing images adorned the walls of temples. His representations with the head of a hawk, always armed and ready for battle, inspired the army to fight with fervor. But the god of war was not the only one to be invoked. Amun-Ra, lord of heaven and earth, also participated in these ceremonies, his energy radiating power and vitality to those who were preparing to face the unknown.

The pharaoh, as intermediary between the gods and the people, was the first to undergo the rites. Gathered with his priests, he entered the sanctuary, where the statue of Montu was anointed with sacred oils and adorned with flowers and offerings. The smell of burning herbs mingled with the aroma of incense, creating an atmosphere charged with mysticism. The priests' chants rose, reverberating between the temple columns and reaching the heavens, where the gods awaited their offerings.

A central part of the ritual included the consecration of weapons. Each sword, spear, and shield was purified in the presence of the gods. The enchantments inscribed on them not only protected them from enemies, but also conferred supernatural strength upon them. Upon touching them, the warriors felt the divine presence running through their hands, as if they were extensions of celestial power. It was said that whoever wielded a weapon consecrated in the name of the gods would not know defeat.

On the banks of the Nile, another ritual unfolded. The generals and commanders of the army were taken to the sacred water, where they partially submerged their weapons and bodies, symbolizing the purification necessary to face the challenges ahead. The Nile, source of life for the Egyptians, now also became the source of victory. With water running down their faces and arms, the army leaders felt renewed and ready for the divine mission that awaited them.

The pharaoh, in a final gesture of devotion, approached the altar and placed the war crown before the divine images. It was a symbolic offering, a reminder that his victory would be a reflection of the favor of the gods, and not just human power. The torches burned more intensely as the leader whispered ancient prayers, asking for protection and the blessing of heaven for himself and his people.

When the rites ended, silence fell upon the temple like a heavy cloak. The gods had spoken through the signs of the ceremony, and the certainty of success permeated the hearts of those present. The army, renewed by divine blessing, marched to the borders, carrying with it the power of Montu and Amun-Ra. For them, war was more than a physical battle - it was a sacred dance, where the fate of kingdoms and civilizations was decided in the spiritual field before manifesting on earth.

When the army returned victorious from the conquered lands, Egypt prepared for the rituals of purification and thanksgiving. The warriors who set foot again on sacred ground knew that the war had left marks not only on their bodies, but also on their souls. Battles, even when favored by the gods, carried with them the shadow of blood and death. Now, it was necessary to restore order, inner peace, and return the conquered lands to spiritual balance.

On the banks of the Nile, the army gathered for one of the most important post-conquest rituals. The priests, dressed in white linen robes, waited to purify the soldiers, their weapons, and the newly acquired lands. At dusk, when the sun began to tinge the sky with shades of gold and orange, the ceremonies began. Each warrior plunged into the sacred water of the river, washing not only the dust of battle, but also the spiritual remnants of the deaths and confrontations experienced. The Nile, always associated with renewal and life, was seen as the element capable of cleansing any trace of disorder brought about by wars.

While the army purified itself in the waters, in the temple of Amun-Ra, the pharaoh and his priests conducted the thanksgiving rituals. The images of the gods, wrapped in fragrances of myrrh and incense, received offerings in the form of fruits, flowers, and hand-carved statuettes, representing the victory and prosperity that the pharaoh had secured for his people. The priests chanted songs, and the echo of these voices traveled through the temple columns, rising to the heavens, where the gods awaited their gratitude.

But purification was not complete without the consecration of the conquered lands. For the Egyptians, each piece of land carried its own spiritual essence, and the new territory, previously inhabited by other peoples, needed to be reordered according to the cosmic forces of Ma'at. The pharaoh, accompanied by his generals and priests, traveled to the limits of the new frontiers. There, a temporary altar was erected, where offerings were made. With his hands raised to the sky, the leader recited sacred formulas, asking the gods to accept that land as part of the Egyptian kingdom, and that divine harmony be restored upon it.

In addition to offerings, a symbolic act was performed: the newly conquered land was washed with water from the Nile, carried in jars carefully kept for this occasion. By wetting the ground with the sacred water, the priests ensured that the spirit of fertility and prosperity would flow there, blessing the new territory and those who would inhabit it. Everything was enveloped in a reverent silence, where the sound of water falling on the ground mingled with the prayers murmured by those present.

At the end of the ceremonies, a great celebration took place. The people gathered to give thanks and celebrate the victory. The markets were filled with life, dancers and musicians paid homage to the gods with movements and melodies that reverberated through the squares and avenues. During these festivals, it was common for gold and silver statuettes, representing the gods of war and fertility, to be distributed among army leaders and prominent officers, as a way of recognizing the divine favor that accompanied them during battle.

Thus, the cycle of conquest was completed. It was not just a matter of military or political expansion; it was a process in which the spiritual and the earthly intertwined. The gods were present at every step, from preparation for war to the consecration of conquered lands. The pharaoh, mediator between heaven and earth, ensured that the cosmic balance was maintained and that, through complex and profound rituals, Egypt continued under the protection and grace of the deities it so revered.

Chapter 16
Rituals of Communication with Ancestors

As dusk approached, a cloak of reverent silence covered the villages and cities along the banks of the Nile. The soft sound of the waters flowed like a distant murmur, while families began to prepare for one of the most sacred and deeply respected rituals in Ancient Egypt: communication with the spirits of ancestors. There was an unshakeable belief that death did not completely sever the ties between the living and the dead. On the contrary, the ancestors remained present, observing, guiding, and even intervening in the world of the living.

On nights like this, where the stars seemed closer, the "Festival of Wag" marked the beginning of the connection with those who had departed. During this time, families gathered in cemeteries or sacred places to pay homage to their ancestors, lighting small flames that served as beacons, guiding the spirits back to the world of the living. At the center of each altar, an offering: breads, fruits, and wine, carefully arranged alongside protective statues, such as those of Isis and Osiris, the guardians of the transition between life and death.

The murmured prayers were like supplications, laden with deep intentions. The words, though soft, echoed with an invisible force, creating a bridge between the two worlds. Each family believed that, through these rituals, they could not only honor the dead, but also receive guidance and protection from their ancestral spirits. There was always the hope that the ancestors would intervene in important matters, offering advice through signs or dreams. Thus, the spiritual world permeated all aspects of daily life.

In the temples, the priests performed more elaborate ceremonies, invoking the names of illustrious dead, such as ancient pharaohs and great leaders. These rituals, often shrouded in mystery, included chants and the use of sacred texts, written centuries ago. Each name was pronounced with precision, for it was believed that the correct mention of a spirit's name could summon it back to the world of the living, where it could be consulted.

The "Festival of Wag" was just one of the many times when the Egyptians sought this deep connection. In larger temples, such as Karnak or Luxor, the role of oracles was central to these ceremonies. Through oracular methods, such as the throwing of stones or the use of divine statues that seemed to respond to appeals, the living tried to decipher messages from the spirits. The priests, who possessed the gift of mediation, interpreted these signs with the help of the gods.

There was a beauty and harmony in the gestures repeated year after year, and the younger generations learned the importance of keeping the rituals of the ancestors alive. In fact, it was not only about respect for the dead, but about ensuring that the lineage itself continued to flow under the watchful eye of those who once lived.

On deep nights, when the desert wind blew more intensely and silence took over the lands along the banks of the Nile, the Egyptians prepared for the most intimate and enigmatic rituals: direct consultations with the ancestors. It was not uncommon for a family, in times of great decisions or crises, to resort to deeper and more personal methods of communication with the afterlife. The belief that the spirits of the dead could influence events in the world of the living was a force that permeated all layers of Egyptian society, from humble peasants to the highest priests.

These consultation rituals, often conducted by priests with a special connection to the spiritual world, required meticulous preparation. Sacred incenses, prepared with a mixture of resins and desert plants, were burned, creating a dense mist that seemed to open invisible portals between worlds. The smoke, slow and undulating, served as a channel through which the words of the living could reach the spheres where the spirits dwelled.

In the homes of families who maintained this tradition, small protective amulets were placed around the ritual area. The most powerful among them was the "Eye of Horus", a symbol of divine vision, used to ensure that communication was clear and free from evil influences. In front of the altar, specialized priests recited sacred formulas extracted from ancient papyri. The intonation of the words was essential, as it was believed that the correct sound of prayers was as important as their meaning. Each syllable, each sung note, had a specific vibration that resonated in the depths of the spiritual realm.

Magical instruments, such as small polished mirrors and alabaster vases, were also part of this ritual. It was said that the spirits of the ancestors could be reflected in clear surfaces, such as a mirror of water or crystal, and therefore, lotus oil lighting was carefully adjusted to create an environment conducive to apparition. The silence that preceded this moment was almost palpable, as if the air itself were awaiting the ancestral presence.

Once the spirit was invoked, it was not common for it to manifest itself directly. Instead, communication happened subtly: a light breeze blowing through the room, an unexpected noise, or even a vision that appeared in the participants' dreams the following nights. The spirits of the ancestors spoke in symbols and riddles, leaving it to the living to interpret these signs wisely.

Among the oldest and most traditional families, there was the practice of leaving letters or written messages, known as "letters to the dead". These texts, kept in tombs or deposited on altars, served as a direct appeal to the spirits to resolve disputes or protect the house from negative influences. The language of these letters was respectful and, at the same time, full of sincere pleas, expressing the deep belief that the dead still had power over the fate of the living.

The priests, with their ancestral wisdom and mastery of rituals, played a crucial role in this whole process. They were the interpreters, those who understood the whispers of the dead and translated them to the living. Equipped with sacred tools and protected by magic formulas, they invoked the ancestors not just as a memory, but as active and present forces. After all, the Egyptians knew that time was not linear and that the past always influenced the present.

These consultations with the dead were acts of reverence and a search for direction. More than just communication, they symbolized the eternal union between the cycles of life, death, and rebirth, a cycle that the Egyptians believed to be deeply interconnected with the universe as a whole.

Chapter 17
Rituals of Negative Energy Transformation

The Egyptians, masters of the art of interacting with the invisible, believed that the energies around us were malleable. Thus, what seemed like a threat to some, to those who knew the spiritual mysteries, was a force to be transformed. The nature of these energies was seen as a reflection of the cosmic balance that governed everything, and transmutation rituals arose to restore this harmony.

The transformation of negative energy, often associated with unfortunate events or the presence of evil entities, began with a meticulous spiritual evaluation. It was not enough to just identify the source of the disturbance. It was necessary to understand its origin and purpose, as it was believed that all energy carried a message, an echo of human actions or supernatural forces.

To perform these rituals, skilled priests were called to act. In the dim light of the temples, where flickering torches cast eerie shadows on the hieroglyph-adorned walls, they prepared for the sacred process of purification. The first step involved the use of rare incenses, such as frankincense resin and Lebanese cedar, whose smoke was considered capable of unblocking spiritual channels, allowing energy to flow and be transmuted.

The priests chanted ancient songs, sounds that reverberated in harmony with natural forces. Each word uttered was charged with power, imbued with hidden meanings, capable of aligning the spirit with the transforming deities. Thoth, the god of wisdom and magic, was invoked as a guide and mediator. It was he who provided the necessary understanding to navigate the labyrinth of invisible energies and find the point of mutation.

At the center of the altar were placed objects that had been touched by negative energies. These objects were usually talismans, amulets, or even simple stones that, during the ritual, absorbed the evil energies. Once identified, the transmutation process began. The smoke, the chants, and the mental strength of the participants created a current of energy that circulated around these objects, until their evil nature was reversed, transformed into something lighter, more balanced.

The transmutation rituals were not quick. They could last for hours or even days, depending on the intensity of the negative energy involved. The priests remained in deep concentration, as if immersed in an invisible battle, where mind and spirit aligned to bring healing. In addition, it was common for participants to use copper mirrors or crystals to amplify positive vibrations and reflect spiritual light back to the universe.

In the end, the objects that were once carriers of harm were returned to their pure forms. They were washed with the sacred waters of the Nile, a symbol of renewal and life, and buried or offered back to the gods, thus sealing the cycle of purification. For the Egyptians, the ritual of transforming energies was not just a practice of magic, but a constant reminder that everything in life could be healed and reframed, as long as there was wisdom and the touch of the deities.

As the ritual progressed, the deeper secrets of the transmutation process began to emerge. There was something ancestral in the way the priests manipulated invisible forces, transforming chaotic energies into harmony. Around them, the environment seemed to adjust as the ritual progressed, as if the walls of the temples, silent witnesses to centuries of wisdom, were in sync with the power that flowed there.

The ancient texts, carefully kept in the hidden chambers of the temples, revealed specific formulas for different types of negative energies. Each type of evil was faced with its own strategy, and the priests followed these sacred writings with precision. For curses cast by enemies, Thoth and Bastet were called, as both mastered the knowledge of how to untie the spiritual knots that imprisoned life. Bastet, with her feline nature, was the goddess who, with lightness and cunning, cut the bonds of darkness, freeing those who suffered under the influence of evil forces.

The chants, known as the "reversal hymns", were charged with power, a legacy of the stars. It was said that their words were not just sounds, but vibrational frequencies capable of disintegrating the negative and rebuilding balance. Each note and syllable echoed in the temple, causing invisible tremors in the deepest layers of reality. These chants were accompanied by the action of the priests' hands, which, using sacred symbols drawn in the air, weaved an invisible web around the energies to be transformed.

The priests' hands, often adorned with copper rings, followed rehearsed movements that had been passed down for generations. The metal, considered a spiritual conductor, enhanced the rituals by channeling and amplifying the cosmic force that flowed through the bodies of those who dedicated themselves to mystical practice. The rings gleamed under the dim light of the torches, becoming points of light in the shadows of the temple.

There was a special power in the gods summoned for this mission. Thoth, always represented with the head of an ibis, brought mental clarity and a deep understanding of cosmic laws. He not only instructed the priests on how to manipulate negative energy, but also showed the purpose behind each spiritual challenge, allowing suffering to be understood before being dispelled. Bastet, on the other hand, represented protection and healing, her presence calming the souls involved in the ritual, warding off fear and strengthening hearts.

Objects such as the "Eye of Horus" were used as tools of protection and guidance during these rituals. The eye, one of the most powerful amulets in Egypt, was placed at the center of ceremonies to watch over and keep energies under control, ensuring that nothing escaped the sacred circle until it was completely purified. When spiritual light began to shine through the eye, it meant that the transformation was close to completion.

In the end, when the air became lighter and the chants ceased, the priests placed their instruments back on specific altars. The sacred waters of the Nile were sprinkled around the site, sealing the environment and protecting it from new evil influences. With the energy restored, the participants knew they were safe again, free from what had previously tormented them.

The magical texts, engraved on scrolls and walls, made it clear: darkness can only exist until it is touched by the wisdom and power of the gods. The ritual, more than an esoteric practice, was a reminder that light always prevails over chaos, as long as those who walk with the gods know how to invoke it.

Chapter 18
Rituals of Fertility and Agricultural Growth

The soil of Egypt, nourished by the waters of the Nile, carried within it the weight of centuries of offerings and prayers. Each harvest was more than a simple interaction between the land and man—it connected deeply to the realm of the gods. Before any seed was planted, the fields awaited the awakening of the ritual, the call for fertility. It was as if the land were asleep, ready to be touched by divine power, by the invisible hand that nurtured each grain.

The Egyptians knew that agriculture was, above all, a gift from the gods. Min, god of fertility, was one of the main figures venerated by farmers. Always represented in his vigorous form, Min held the scepter that symbolized the life force, and his presence in the fields was requested with great respect. Offerings to Min were placed on altars that flanked the fields, and often consisted of produce from the land, such as the first fruits and grains from the previous season. This symbolized a continuous cycle of giving and gratitude, a sacred exchange between man and the divine.

But it wasn't just the land that needed to be prepared. Before planting began, farmers participated in a purification ritual, bathing in the waters of the Nile.

This water, considered sacred, was used to wash spirits and ensure that no negativity contaminated the sacred soil. After purification, the priests chanted, asking Hapi, the god of the Nile, to bring his waters in an abundant and balanced way, so that the fields would be fertilized without floods or droughts.

The gods of earth and fertility were invoked in different stages. In the beginning, Isis, the divine mother, was called upon to bless the fertility of the land and crops. Farmers believed that she, protector of life, would ensure that the land was ready to receive the seeds, just as a woman prepares to generate life in her womb. Isis was also associated with the rebirth of the seasons and the natural cycle of nature, and her image often adorned the fields, representing renewal.

Min was invoked the moment the seed touched the ground. His power was crucial to ensure that fertility remained firm and that crops grew strong and abundant. During this stage, farmers recited prayers and hymns of thanksgiving, thanking for their life force that permeated the soil and gave life to plants.

The rites included dances around the fields, with rhythmic movements that imitated the cycle of the seasons. The sound of drums, echoing through the valley, awakened the spirit of the earth, as if the gods themselves were descending to the world of mortals to bless the growth of crops. The dances were led by the priests, and the farmers followed their steps, believing that each movement amplified the power of the blessing they were about to receive.

The most sacred moment of the ritual occurred at sunset, when the sky was tinged with gold and red. At this moment, the sacred fire was lit on the stone altars, and the incense, which slowly rose in spirals in the air, carried with it the prayers murmured by the participants. On the altar, small statues of Osiris and Min were positioned, their forms worn by time and past rituals, but charged with an undeniable divine presence. Around them, fruits, flowers and the first harvested wheat served as offerings, reinforcing the pact of fertility between gods and men.

When the ritual drew to a close, the priests used small palm branches to sprinkle Nile water throughout the field, sealing the cycle of blessing. The next morning's dew would be, for them, the final touch of divinity, the sign that the gods had accepted the prayers and that the field would soon flourish with abundance.

The future of the harvest, from then on, depended on the balance between the elements and the maintenance of this sacred connection with the divine. Each dawn, each phase of the moon, would be a reminder that the higher forces were present, awaiting the next offerings and celebrations that would ensure the continuity of life.

In the fertile lands of Egypt, the cycle of harvests was not just an earthly task, but a spiritual dance choreographed by the gods. With the arrival of the planting and harvesting seasons, the spiritual and physical world intertwined in a profound way, and seasonal festivals were a reflection of the incessant search for harmony between man and the forces of nature.

During seasonal festivals, community ceremonies came to life. The Opet festival, for example, which celebrated the god Amun-Ra, was also an agricultural renewal event. Although its most visible aspects were linked to the divine power of the pharaoh, the peasants participated indirectly, offering the first fruits of the work of their hands. The great procession of priests, carrying the sacred statues of Amun, Mut and Khonsu, passed by the banks of the Nile, and the people gathered, leaving offerings and praying for a bountiful harvest and protection from pests and natural disasters.

However, the festival most directly linked to fertility was the "Festival of the Nile". This took place at the height of summer, when the waters of the great river began to rise, bringing with them the rich, fertile mud that nourished the fields. For the Egyptian people, the Nile was not just a river, but the lifeblood of their entire civilization, and Hapi, its spirit, was venerated with extreme devotion.

During the festival, priests performed rituals on the banks of the Nile, dipping sacred vessels into the waters and bringing the spiritual life of the river to the temples and fields. Small papyrus boats, laden with offerings and clay figures representing the gods, were launched into the waters in a delicate ceremony. The movement of the boats, floating with the current, was seen as a dialogue between the people and the river, a silent request for the waters to return in abundance and fertility.

The people communed with the priests, offering fruits, vegetables and wine. The purification, which had begun in the field, was now completed by the water of the Nile, which bathed the banks and carried with it any trace of bad luck or infertility. The return of the flood was awaited with mystical anxiety, as its arrival not only brought fertility to the soil, but also marked the time for new offerings to be made.

Fertility prayers were recited in unison, asking that the river remain generous, that the flood be neither too much nor too little, and that the cycle of life could continue in balance. Small images of Min, made of clay, were buried on the banks of the fields, a symbolic act of planting the very essence of fertility in the earth. These figures carried the strength of the god, and as they decomposed, they released, it was believed, the energy necessary for plants to grow vigorously.

Collective ceremonies not only reinforced the union between farmers and the divine, but were also a time for strengthening community ties. Families worked together to build the temporary altars that lined the fields, decorated with the first flowers of the season. While offerings were being made, ancient chants filled the air, transporting the minds and hearts of the participants to the spiritual realms.

The priests, dressed in white robes, symbolizing purity and renewal, conducted the rites with firmness. It was they who knew the specific enchantments for each season, for each harvest. The use of appropriate magical formulas was vital, as the balance between the elements and the divine response depended on the precision of the rituals. Each word uttered was a key, opening doors between the earthly and spiritual worlds.

Among the consecrated techniques, a special practice was reserved for times of drought or threat to the harvest: the invocation of the winds. Through sacred chants, the priests asked the god Shu to bring cool breezes to spread the moisture of the Nile over the fields, preventing drought and ensuring the nourishment of plants. If the invocation was successful, gentle winds swept through the valley, and the people believed that the gods were directly intervening.

Another essential aspect of fertility rituals was the consecration of agricultural tools. Plows, sickles and baskets were blessed by the priests before being used in the harvest, ensuring they were imbued with divine energy. Wood and metal, carefully prepared, were seen as an extension of the life force of the gods, a means by which human work could align with the spiritual plane.

Finally, the culmination of the abundance rituals was the "harvest dance", a frantic and joyful celebration, where men and women danced to the sound of flutes and drums. The land, already blessed, responded with promises of abundance, and the sweat of the farmers became part of the sacred cycle, mingling with the soil as a final tribute.

And so, Egypt lived the eternal cycle of life, death and rebirth, in which the simple act of planting and harvesting was always intertwined with divine mysteries, with cosmic balance, and with the intimate relationship between man, the soil, and the gods.

Chapter 19
Rituals of Peace and Harmony

The ancient Egyptians understood that, for their lives to flow in balance, it was essential to maintain a deep and continuous relationship with the concept of Ma'at, the personification of cosmic order, justice, and truth. Rituals aimed at peace and harmony were not limited to personal needs, but were also practices of collective responsibility, where the balance between the physical and spiritual worlds should be maintained at all costs.

In times of disorder, both within the kingdom and between neighboring nations, the people resorted to the temples, seeking in the silence of the gods the answers to restore balance. The image of Ma'at, with her ostrich feather, was placed on the altar, beside the carefully arranged offerings: wine, bread, fruits, and incense. The priests, with their eyes turned towards the desert horizon, knew that the very existence of the kingdom depended on the order established by the gods. Thus, invocations were made with deep reverence.

In ceremonies conducted within the temples of Amun-Ra and Ptah, gods known for their connection to creation and harmony, the priests began the ritual with an act of purification. They dipped their hands in stone basins filled with water taken directly from the Nile, consecrated for being the river that connected human life to the divine plane. After purification, the chanting began, and each word chanted was an offering to the goddess of order, an attempt to align human thoughts and actions with the higher forces that governed the universe.

The enchantments for peace were soft, like a breeze cutting through the silence of the prayer room. The words floated in the air, and there was a sense of collective expectation, as if the temple space itself was waiting for a divine response. The ancients believed that chaos, symbolized by Seth, was an ever-present force, ready to manifest if not carefully kept under control by rituals and offerings.

Among the objects used in these rites, small amulets of jade and alabaster stood out, engraved with the image of Ma'at and distributed among the participants. It was believed that these talismans not only offered protection, but also brought harmony to those who carried them, linking them directly to the spirit of the goddess. With each prayer recited, these amulets absorbed the energy of the ritual, becoming channels between the material and spiritual worlds.

In times of greatest disorder, when peace seemed distant, more elaborate rituals were performed. The pharaoh, considered the intermediary between the gods and men, took an active part in pacification ceremonies, in which the divine power of the crown became essential. Dressed in the insignia of Horus, the ruler went to the temple sanctuary, where, in a solemn procession, he offered sacrifices to seal the peace. The offerings were accompanied by solemn oaths, written on scrolls and recited aloud, ensuring that the intentions of peace would prevail among those involved.

The act of bringing harmony was not restricted to times of war. The Egyptians knew that true peace must begin within their own homes and communities. When there were family disagreements or conflicts between neighbors, families resorted to domestic rituals. Women were often the guardians of domestic harmony, and used small altars in their homes to invoke Hathor, the goddess of love and beauty, asking for reconciliation and understanding.

At such times, it was common for an earthenware bowl, filled with scented oil and lotus flowers, to be placed in a prominent place in the home, where everyone could see and smell the sweet perfume of the prayers raised.

The prayers recited in these domestic rituals were simple, but laden with symbolism. Sometimes the words were not spoken aloud, but whispered or even thought, as if the act of internalization were enough to communicate the needs of the heart directly to the gods. It was a reminder that true peace came from within, and that external forces could only be controlled when inner balance was restored.

Public celebrations, such as the Heb-Sed Festival, were times when the entire nation sought renewal and harmony. During this festival, which marked the renewal of the pharaoh's strength and legitimacy, the population gathered in processions, carrying symbolic offerings, from baskets of fruit to small clay idols. These figures, sculpted in the shapes of gods and sacred animals, were left at the foot of the great altars in ceremonies that lasted for days.

At the end of the rites, when the temple was filled with the aroma of incense and the voices of the priests had fallen silent, the people returned to their homes, believing that peace had been restored. In the days that followed, the flow of life continued, with the certainty that the gods had heard their pleas and that harmony prevailed, at least for another cycle of seasons.

Egypt thus lived between balance and chaos, but always seeking peace as a reflection of the universal order imposed by the gods.

In the stillness of the temples, where the twilight cast shadows that seemed to have a life of their own, the most complex rituals of peace and harmony unfolded. These were times when not only the nation, but the cosmos itself seemed to be at stake. The temple became a microcosm of the universe, and every gesture of the priests, every word uttered, carried the weight of the cosmic order.

Major crises, whether political or spiritual, required a level of divine intervention that only the oldest and most powerful gods could offer. The pharaoh, in his capacity as direct representative of the gods, conducted the rituals alongside the high priests. He wore the sacred symbols that denoted his position: the scepter and the ankh, the first representing power and the second eternal life. The circle that surrounded them was sacred, and within it, invisible forces moved, responding to the appeals of mortals.

Inside the temple, the walls adorned with engravings told stories of other times, when the gods walked side by side with men, guiding them along paths of peace and prosperity. Each ceremony was an attempt to recapture this lost harmony, invoking the divine presence to correct what had been broken.

The ceremony began with an offering of incense, the same that was believed to have been used to please the gods since the beginning of time. The aroma of incense had the power to lift prayers to the spiritual world, making the connection between the earthly and celestial planes tangible. The priests, with precise and calculated movements, let the incense rise to the sky, drawing invisible spirals that danced with the wind, while murmuring words of power.

The chants, chanted in unison, echoed through the sacred space, reverberating through the gigantic columns and altars, impregnated by the presence of the gods. It was believed that these words, repeated for generations, carried an accumulated power, as if each recitation reinforced the bonds between man and the divine. The texts that the priests read were kept secret, passed down from generation to generation as a sacred treasure. They contained clear instructions on how to restore harmony in times of crisis, invoking gods like Ptah, creator of the world, and Horus, symbol of royalty and victory over chaos.

At more delicate moments, when social harmony was in jeopardy, the priests performed ritualistic judgments. In these, the temple was transformed into a sacred court, where the laws of Ma'at prevailed. The participants, both accusers and accused, were subjected to a divine test. Truth was not just an abstract concept, but a living force that guided the process. The feather of Ma'at, symbol of justice, was present, and at the end of the trial, only the purest hearts prevailed.

These trials were not just to resolve earthly disputes. It was believed that imbalance in the human world reflected an imbalance in the cosmos. Therefore, the restoration of peace was not merely an act of justice, but a correction of the very fabric of the universe. The verdict was given by the priests, who, through their prayers and invocations, sought guidance directly from the gods.

To ensure that the peace achieved was lasting, protective amulets were distributed at the end of the ceremony. These objects, usually made of precious stones or rare metals, contained sacred symbols and were consecrated during the ritual. They were more than just adornments: they represented the constant presence of the gods in the lives of the Egyptians, ensuring that peace was maintained and that chaos was kept at bay.

Communities, in turn, held their own celebrations of peace and harmony, especially during seasonal festivals. These festivals were times of collective renewal, where it was believed that the cycle of nature could be harmonized with the cycle of human life. During the Opet Festival, for example, the pharaoh led a grand procession, carrying the statues of the gods Amun, Mut and Khonsu through the streets of the city.

The people gathered in celebration, with offerings, music and dance, in a ritual that symbolized the union between the gods and humans, bringing harmony to the nation.

In homes, families also participated in this quest for harmony. In the simplest homes, small altars were set up to receive divine blessings. Each house had its own rhythm of prayers, its own rituals, but the ultimate goal was always the same: to ensure that order prevailed over chaos. Mothers were often the first to light the incense, while the elders recited the sacred words learned from their ancestors.

It was common that, at the end of a long period of chaos, a larger offering was made on behalf of the entire community. An animal, usually an ox or a goat, was sacrificed, and its blood spilled on sacred ground. This act represented the reestablishment of the alliance between man and the divine, a renewed pact that ensured peace and the continuity of life.

Thus, the rituals of peace and harmony transcended the human plane, reaching the highest spheres of the universe. They were not just moments of devotion, but were the very essence of Egyptian life, a life that balanced between order and chaos, always seeking the eternal blessing of Ma'at, the goddess who kept everything in perfect harmony.

Chapter 20
Rituals for the Protection of Children and Families

The protection of family life in ancient Egypt was a sacred aspect, enveloped in ancestral rituals that connected the home to protective deities. Each family sought, through daily rituals and more elaborate ceremonies, to ensure that their children and homes were surrounded by divine forces, warding off the evil that dwelled in the shadows. The family environment, seen as a reflection of cosmic harmony, required constant balance, where the power of magic and divine blessings were evoked to maintain this order.

In villages and cities, it was not uncommon to see mothers preparing small altars in their homes. At the center, there was always the protective figure of Hathor or Bes, two deities deeply connected to family protection. Hathor, the goddess of love and motherhood, was frequently invoked to protect newborns and ensure their healthy growth. Bes, the god of peculiar appearance, with grotesque features, was the protector of children, warding off evil spirits and plagues that could affect them.

Upon birth, children received talismans that would protect them throughout their lives. The "Isis knot", for example, was an amulet commonly placed around the necks of little ones, symbolizing the bond between mother, child, and the mystical powers of the goddess. It was as if, by carrying this symbol, children were directly connected to the maternal and protective force of Isis, becoming invisible to the lurking negative forces.

Parents, in turn, had their own rituals. Every year, during the festival of Bastet, they took offerings to the temples of the cat goddess, known for her ability to protect against disease and disaster. Bastet, with her penetrating eyes and feline nature, was invoked to watch over homes, ensuring that no calamity befell them. The offerings, composed of flowers, fruits, and small cat-shaped artifacts, were left on the altars while chants and prayers ascended to the sky, asking for continued protection.

Within homes, incense was a constant element. The fragrance that spread through the rooms not only purified but also functioned as an invisible shield against negative energies. Priests guided families on the best incenses to use: sandalwood, which brought peace and harmony, or myrrh, used to expel evil spirits. The smoke that rose to the heavens carried with it the silent prayers of mothers and fathers, who wished for the safety of their children and the unity of their homes.

The birth of a child was a deeply ritualistic moment. As soon as the child arrived in the world, it was bathed in consecrated water, usually taken from the Nile River, considered the source of life. The water, blessed by the priests, purified the body and spirit of the newborn, marking it as protected by the gods. This first bath was not a simple act of hygiene, but a ritual of initiation into life, an introduction to the spiritual path that every Egyptian should follow from the moment they first breathed.

The rituals of protection were not limited to birth or the first years of life. Throughout childhood, children underwent a series of rites of passage, where additional amulets were introduced and more powerful prayers were recited. In the days leading up to the onset of puberty, for example, parents ordered special amulets, such as the "eye of Horus", which should be worn to ward off envy and the ill intentions of others. This symbol, associated with the omnipresent vision of Horus, the falcon god, ensured that the child was always under divine surveillance.

As the child grew, the family gathered in periodic ceremonies, where food and small symbolic objects were offered to the gods in exchange for continued protection. These family gatherings, always held with great reverence, reminded everyone of the fragility of life and the need to keep the gods close, especially those who watched over the integrity of children.

In Egyptian society, the family was not just a social unit, but a reflection of the cosmos itself. Chaos, symbolized by the absence of divine protection, was a constant threat, and only the maintenance of rituals could ensure that homes remained in harmony with the universe. For this, each family member had a role to play: the father as head of the household and intermediary with the gods, the mother as guardian of the home and children, and the children, who from an early age learned to respect and participate in the ceremonies that would protect them throughout their lives.

Within this continuous cycle of protection, Egypt flourished, a reflection of the cosmic order maintained not only in the grand temples but also in the heart of each home, where deities coexisted daily with mortals, ensuring peace, health, and prosperity for each family.

The preservation of the family nucleus in ancient Egypt was not limited to protection against physical dangers. There was a deep concern for the spiritual integrity of family members. The rituals performed to ensure that both body and spirit were protected were elaborated with meticulousness, reflecting the fear of invisible forces that could destabilize homes.

On the banks of the Nile, when the night wind blew, stories circulated about vengeful spirits and family curses, which could last for generations. To prevent the manifestation of these forces, the Egyptians resorted to specific rituals to protect their descendants from harmful influences. One of the most notorious rituals involved the use of the Isis knot, tied with a red ribbon around the wrists of children. This color, in addition to symbolizing vital power, was considered a barrier against the evil eye and evil spirits that wandered among the living.

Annual festivities also carried with them auspicious moments for the protection of families. The festival of Wag, one of the most significant, was a period when the dead were honored, and families offered food and small artifacts in their tombs to appease their spirits and ensure that, from beyond, they continued to watch over their descendants. There was no clear line between the world of the living and the world of the dead in the Egyptian imagination; both were deeply intertwined, and the spiritual protection of ancestors was essential for the maintenance of family harmony.

One of the most recurrent practices during these celebrations was the recitation of ancient enchantments, passed down from generation to generation. These words, kept secret by families and repeated in moments of great importance, were charged with power, connecting the living to ancient traditions and the gods who watched over family well-being. Mothers often taught these chants to their children, ensuring that the knowledge of spiritual protection was not lost over time.

In times of illness or weakness, the Egyptians believed that negative energies could lodge in the body, especially in children, who were seen as more vulnerable to these forces. To ward off these influences, the use of talismans was common, but not sufficient. There were specific fumigation rituals, where sacred herbs, such as mugwort and frankincense, were burned inside houses, purifying the environment and bodies. The priests of Anubis, the jackal god associated with protection and guide in the underworld, were called to supervise these rituals, ensuring that the spiritual cleansing process was complete and that evil energies were banished.

In addition to purification practices, there were rituals aimed at fortifying homes. An example of this was the construction of talismans in the form of sacred animals, such as the cats of Bastet, which were placed in each corner of the house. These talismans had the power to attract the benevolence of the gods and ward off evil spirits that might try to invade the sacred space of the family. In times of calamity, such as floods or plagues, families gathered around these talismans and recited prayers while placing small sacred objects at the feet of the statues, sealing a pact of protection with the gods.

Another fundamental ritual for family protection was performed in temples during the festivals dedicated to Horus. The eye of Horus, one of the most powerful amulets in the Egyptian imagination, symbolized divine protection and constant vigilance against invisible dangers. The priests, in grand ceremonies, consecrated new amulets, which were distributed among the devotees and their families, ensuring that the protection of the falcon god extended over homes throughout the year.

As children grew, new rites of passage were performed. The transition to adulthood, especially for boys, involved rituals where family protection was reinforced, now not just as a passive blessing, but as a power to be actively carried. Young people were taught to invoke the gods, to recognize divine signs, and to protect their future homes with the same zeal that their parents had done before. For girls, rites of passage involved offerings to Hathor and Isis, ensuring fertility, protection during childbirth, and harmony in marriage.

Marriage, in turn, was one of the most crucial moments for the continuity of spiritual protection within the family. The union of two families meant the fusion of two spiritual universes, and the rituals performed before and during the wedding sought not only to ensure marital happiness but also to protect future descendants from any cosmic curse or disharmony that could be inherited. During wedding ceremonies, amulets were exchanged between the bride and groom, and priests recited incantations to seal the union under the eyes of Horus, making the new home a reflection of divine harmony.

Spiritual protection, for the Egyptians, was a constant dance between the visible and the invisible, between the present and the eternal. The rituals, complex and laden with symbolism, not only protected families from immediate threats but also ensured that future generations inherited a legacy of security and harmony, deeply intertwined with the forces of the cosmos and the will of the gods. The cycle of protection, like the flow of the Nile, never ceased.

Chapter 21
Rituals of Social and Political Transformation

On the banks of the Nile, power flowed like the river itself, and the rituals that sustained this current were vital to the survival of a civilization that saw in its rulers the bridge between gods and mortals. In Ancient Egypt, the coronation of a pharaoh was much more than a political ceremony; it was an event of cosmic proportions. Upon assuming the throne, the pharaoh not only inherited the physical kingdom but also the responsibility to maintain divine order, Ma'at, ensuring harmony between heaven and earth.

This carefully orchestrated moment began with the ritual isolation of the future ruler. In a sacred temple, far from the eyes of the people, the new pharaoh underwent days of purification, bathing in consecrated waters and receiving blessings from priests who invoked the protection of Amon-Ra, the king of the gods. Physical purification was only the beginning of a spiritual transformation, where the pharaoh would gradually become a living deity.

The chants of the priests echoed through the temple walls, and with them, the secret name of the pharaoh, the name that only he and the gods knew, was whispered to the winds. This name was the true power that allowed him not only to rule but to transcend the material world. Once revealed, it carried with it the destiny of Egypt, the key that would maintain order and ward off chaos.

Upon emerging from this period of isolation, the pharaoh was presented to the people as a renewed figure, surrounded by the symbols of divine power. The double crown, which united Upper and Lower Egypt, was placed upon his head, representing the union of the two kingdoms and the restored harmony. But this physical symbol concealed an even deeper meaning: the fusion of the human with the divine, the transformation of the ruler into an intermediary between the gods and mortals.

During the coronation ceremony, the pharaoh made offerings in temples throughout the country. He, now deified, offered himself to the gods as the perfect servant, guaranteeing them eternal devotion in exchange for prosperity and protection for his kingdom. The statues of the gods were adorned with jewels and gold, while sacred incense filled the air, creating a dense atmosphere, imbued with mystery and power.

But it was not only the pharaoh who underwent a transformation. The people of Egypt were also part of this ritual. The ascension of a new ruler signified a renewal of the covenant between the people and the gods. Festivals were held in all cities, large and small, where offerings were made and prayers were raised to heaven. The Egyptians, believers in the power of words and ritual action, knew that their participation was essential to maintain the cosmic balance.

As the new pharaoh walked through the temple of Karnak, followed by his priests and advisors, he repeated the gestures of his predecessors. He held the heka scepter and the nekhakha crook, symbols of power and protection, in his hands, while reciting the hymns that invoked the presence of the gods. With each step, the invisible world opened before him, and his connection to the divine strengthened.

In the days following the coronation, political rituals took shape, where the pharaoh reaffirmed his commitment to justice and order. Ancient disputes between nobles were resolved, laws were proclaimed, and the first offerings to the Nile were made to ensure an abundant and prosperous flood. The ruler, now a divine avatar, became the living manifestation of Ma'at, and his reign would be judged by how well he maintained this delicate balance between the forces of chaos and order.

And so, Egypt, guided by its new ruler, followed its course in the mystical waters of time, protected by the blessings of the gods, with the certainty that cosmic harmony, restored by rituals of power, ensured the future of the kingdom. The sound of drums echoed throughout the valley, and sunlight bathed the temples, gilding the sacred stones that sustained the kingdom. The festivities that followed the coronation were not merely celebrations; they represented the renewal of an eternal cycle, where power passed from the hands of the gods to the pharaoh. The people danced and sang, in a collective trance, aware that their prosperity depended on the spiritual strength of the new leader. The throne had been occupied, but the ritual was far from over.

In the heart of the temple, the priests whispered ancestral enchantments as the pharaoh approached the altar, where the statue of Amon-Ra shone in the light of hundreds of oil lamps. This moment was vital: the reaffirmation of his union with the gods, of his legitimacy as heir to the cosmic power that governed both the earthly and spiritual worlds.

By raising the scepter before the gods, the pharaoh made a silent promise, a promise to maintain order, to protect the people, and to preserve the balance between the worlds. This oath was sealed with precious offerings: gold, rare stones, and the best grains from the fertile land of the Nile. Each offering represented a request, and each request was made not for self-benefit, but for the continuity of the cycle of abundance that kept Egypt prosperous.

The festivals were a spectacle of devotion, where not only the pharaoh but the entire court reaffirmed their role. The elites, nobles, and high priests gathered to make their own offerings, aware that their loyalty to the pharaoh was intrinsically linked to their destiny. Political power flowed from a spiritual source, and the gods watched closely, ensuring that no link in the chain was broken.

Beyond the temple walls, the celebration echoed in the streets. The people believed that during these days, harmony spread like a divine breath, restoring homes, fertilizing the land, and bringing temporary peace. In this climate, everyone, from the humblest peasants to the wealthiest merchants, participated in the cycle of renewal, in a symphony of faith and hope.

However, among the public rituals, there were those that were more secret. In the most hidden chambers of the temple, only those initiated into the mysteries of politics and spirituality knew the enchantments that sealed the pact between the pharaoh and the gods. There, the oracles were consulted. In the silence of these rooms, the future was read, and decisions about war, alliances, and the conduct of the kingdom were made based on visions that transcended reality. Power came not only from military strength or economic wealth but from access to this hidden knowledge, from the ability to interpret the signs sent by the gods.

Foreign rulers also made their offerings, seeking favors, alliances, and protection from the powerful throne of Egypt. Such rituals were not merely a demonstration of respect; they were, above all, a spiritual negotiation, where the balance of political power in the Mediterranean and beyond depended on the acceptance of the Egyptian gods.

As the rituals progressed, the pharaoh became more than an earthly ruler. He became the axis of the cosmos, the point of connection between the divine and the human. The blessings of Amon-Ra were transferred to his body, and his authority was legitimized by the celestial order, reaffirmed by rites that protected Egypt from any disorder or chaos.

With the end of the festivities, the pharaoh was now consecrated as the true son of the gods. His royalty was no longer just a physical mantle but a spiritual, immortal essence that would echo in every decision, in every battle, and in every judgment made during his reign.

Chapter 22
Preparation Rituals for the Afterlife

From their first breath, Egyptians lived under the shadow of the afterlife. In Egyptian thought, death did not represent the end, but a delicate transition, an arduous journey toward spiritual rebirth. Preparing for this journey was crucial, not only in the final moments of life but from the very first steps. Each stage of existence, from birth to old age, represented a series of silent rites that prepared the body and spirit for the inevitable encounter with the gods of the underworld.

The tomb, a dwelling for eternity, was the first essential element in preparing for death. Even before falling ill or feeling the weight of years, individuals of higher status began the construction of their tombs. These monuments were not just mortuary chambers, but reflections of the journey to come. The architecture of the tomb was meticulously planned to symbolize the passage through the underworld, with passages that imitated the paths the soul should follow. Detailed engravings of enchantments, especially those taken from the Book of the Dead, adorned the inner walls, serving as a guide and protection. The goal was clear: to ensure that the spirit, upon passing through the trials of the other world, would find its way to Aaru, the paradise where the soul would live in peace, surrounded by reed fields and tranquil waters.

The physical preparation of the body, through the embalming process, was intrinsically linked to spiritual destiny. Embalmers, often compared to priests, performed a ritual of transformation. By preserving the body, it was believed that the deceased's spiritual identity was preserved. The process of removing internal organs and subsequent mummification was laden with symbolism: the heart, left in the body, was seen as the receptacle of emotions and morality, crucial for the judgment that would take place in the Hall of Ma'at. The brain, considered less important for the afterlife, was discarded, skillfully removed through the nostrils.

Along with the body, a series of objects accompanied the deceased in their tomb. Amulets, such as the heart scarab, were strategically positioned between the mummy's bandages. These small artifacts, each with a specific purpose, were a guarantee of protection and luck in the spiritual crossing. The scarab, in particular, had the function of preventing the deceased's heart from testifying against them during the judgment of Osiris. For, in the Hall of Two Truths, where the soul would be confronted with its deeds in life, only those with hearts as light as a feather could proceed to eternal life.

The ritual of the opening of the mouth, conducted by the priests, was one of the most significant during the funeral. Performed in front of the tomb, this ritual allowed the deceased to breathe, speak, and eat again in the afterlife, guaranteeing them a full existence after death. With a sacred instrument, the priest touched the mouth and eyes of the mummy, symbolically restoring the senses and preparing the spirit for the next phase of its journey. At the same time, chants echoed, invoking the gods to bless the deceased and open the doors of the underworld.

These rituals, performed with precision and devotion, were accompanied by offerings. Food, drinks, and flowers were deposited in the tomb, not only to nourish the body of the deceased but also to nourish their spirit. The continuity of these offerings over the years was vital, ensuring that the deceased was not forgotten by the living and that their soul remained strong in the afterlife.

Another fundamental aspect of this preparation involved the ka and the ba, the two spiritual forces that made up the human being. While the ka represented vital energy and should be kept nourished with offerings in the tomb, the ba, the part of the soul capable of wandering between the world of the living and the dead, needed ritual care to ensure that its transition was smooth. For the Egyptians, harmony between these two forces was essential for the deceased to find true peace in the afterlife.

The role of sacred texts in preparing for the afterlife could not be underestimated. Many Egyptians, especially those of the upper classes, ensured that passages from the Book of the Dead were inscribed on their sarcophagi and tomb walls. These texts were not just prayers or chants but true spiritual maps. Each enchantment aimed to protect the deceased at a specific point in the journey, helping them to overcome monsters, traps, and challenges imposed by the gods of the underworld. Without these texts, the soul ran the risk of getting lost in the depths of the Duat, the dark realm of the dead, or worse, being devoured by Ammit, the monster that awaited the condemned.

Even the gods had a vital role in this preparation process. Isis and Nephthys, the goddesses who mourned the death of Osiris, were often invoked at funerals to protect the deceased in the same way they protected their brother. Horus, son of Osiris, was another central god, representing victory over death and ensuring that the cycle of rebirth would be complete.

These rituals, imbued with mystery and reverence, were a reminder that life, for the Egyptians, was not an end point but a continuous passage, where the spirit encountered new challenges and new hopes. Each offering, each enchantment, each gesture performed by the living had an echo in the afterlife, shaping the spiritual journey of their loved ones. Preparation for the afterlife, then, was a refined art, a dance with eternity where past, present, and future intertwined.

In the deep halls of the afterlife, where Osiris reigns and souls face their greatest judgments, preparation is the shield of the spirit. The heart, a symbol of a lifetime's actions, will be placed on the scales, and before it will be the feather of Ma'at, the goddess of truth and justice. This is the crucial moment where every detail, every ritual, culminates. The lightness of the heart determines whether the soul will be condemned to darkness or reborn in the fields of Aaru, where the sun shines eternally.

For many, the moment of weighing was the most feared. They knew that their actions in life, however small, would be revealed. Therefore, the magic of the sacred texts, especially the Book of the Dead, was an indispensable tool. The enchantments contained therein offered protection against errors in judgment. One of the most important texts instructed the heart not to betray its owner, clamoring for the deceased to be absolved before Osiris and his 42 judges. These gods, representing different aspects of truth and justice, formed an imposing barrier, but with the right words, the deceased could appease them.

The offerings deposited next to the tomb were not only for the body but also to spiritually nourish the ka, the vital essence that would continue to exist in the afterlife. In the world of the living, the deceased's family maintained regular rituals, presenting food and drink, believing that in this way they maintained a connection with the spirit. Death did not break the bonds; it transcended them. In due time, the living would also make their journey to the Duat, and together they could reunite.

Among the most crucial elements of the spiritual journey, the ba, the soul capable of traveling between worlds, needed to return to the tomb at night, resting in the mummified body. This symbolic return represented the eternal cycle of death and rebirth. To ensure that the ba did not get lost, specific amulets and enchantments were inserted into the folds of the mummy's bandages.

One of the most powerful was the djed, pillar of Osiris, which symbolized stability and regeneration, reinforcing the cycle of the soul's return.

And in the midst of all this, there was a key character: Anubis, the jackal-headed god. He, the guardian of the necropolis, led the deceased safely through the portals of the Duat. He was the figure who supervised the embalming and who stood beside the scales in the Hall of Two Truths. His penetrating gaze, engraved in many tombs, ensured that the process was followed according to divine laws. Under his protection, the deceased's heart would find justice or condemnation.

Ammit, the devourer, remained in the shadows, patiently awaiting the hearts that would fail in the weighing. This monster, part lion, part crocodile, and part hippopotamus, was the personification of the fear that haunted the Egyptians. The complete annihilation of the soul was the fate of those who failed the judgment. A fate worse than death, for it meant the end of existence in all its forms.

The rituals to ensure a light heart and a protected spirit began long before death. The individual lived a moral life, following the precepts of Ma'at. Throughout the days, prayers and rites were performed, seeking to maintain harmony between body, mind, and the universe. The deceased, before Osiris, would have to proclaim their innocence in a negative confession, listing the sins they did not commit: "I did not steal, I did not lie, I did not kill." Each word, a step closer to salvation.

These rites, subtly intertwined with daily practices and deep beliefs about the cosmos, transformed the moment of death into a grand event, a rebirth.

Chapter 23
Death Rituals and the Passage to the Afterlife

The crossing to the afterlife, in ancient Egypt, was seen as one of the most decisive moments of existence. Death was not an end, but the beginning of a complex journey, a crossing through dark lands filled with spiritual challenges that culminated in the judgment of the soul. For the Egyptians, earthly life was a constant preparation for this moment. And this preparation involved sacred rituals, intended to ensure that the soul could pass through the portals of the underworld, the Duat, and achieve eternal life alongside the gods.

Death rituals began long before the last breath. The process of passage to the afterlife involved a series of carefully executed ceremonies, where each detail had a profound meaning. When a person died, the body was immediately prepared to be purified and embalmed, ensuring that the soul could follow its path without being trapped in the physical world. This purification was not merely physical; it was a spiritual act, where the integrity of the body was crucial for rebirth in the afterlife. Thus, embalmers were seen as priests, who guided the dead in their first step towards the eternal.

The embalming process, often conducted in secret chambers, was surrounded by mysteries. Horus and Anubis, protector gods of the passage to the afterlife, were invoked to bless the body. Anubis, the jackal-headed god, was the guardian of the dead and responsible for ensuring that the embalming was carried out correctly. He also protected the body from evil spirits that might try to divert the soul from its path. During the process, vital organs were carefully removed and preserved in canopic jars, each protected by a son of Horus, symbolizing that the body would continue to be protected in the afterlife.

But the protection of the body was only the beginning. The heart, considered the center of the soul and emotions, was treated with special care. In Egyptian death rituals, the heart was not removed, as it was believed that it would be judged before Osiris at the most critical moment of the soul's journey. The "weighing of the heart" would be the culmination of the crossing through the Duat, when the heart would be placed on a scale against the feather of Ma'at, goddess of truth and justice. If the heart was lighter than or equal to the feather, it meant that the person had lived a just and balanced life, allowing their soul to continue its journey. Otherwise, it would be devoured by Ammit, the fearsome creature that waited to consume impure souls, leading them to annihilation.

Funeral rituals also included the creation of funerary masks, which were placed over the face of the deceased. These masks, often made of gold or painted with vibrant colors, were not just adornments. They had a mystical role: they symbolized the connection between the dead and the divine. The use of the mask allowed the deceased to be recognized by the gods in the afterlife. It was a way to ensure that the soul did not get lost on its journey and could be identified and welcomed by Osiris and the other gods. The masks were carefully decorated with sacred symbols, which reinforced this protection and guided the soul in the unknown.

Throughout this preparation, sacred texts were often inscribed on the sarcophagus or the walls of the tomb, offering detailed instructions for the soul during its passage through the Duat. These texts, known as the "Pyramid Texts" and, later, the "Book of the Dead," were spiritual guides, where enchantments, prayers, and magic formulas were recorded. The deceased was to recite these words before the gods and demons of the underworld, overcoming challenges and avoiding traps that could divert their soul from the right path. Each enchantment was carefully chosen to ensure that the soul was prepared for what it would encounter on the other side.

The presence of amulets was essential in funeral rituals. They were placed on the embalmed body, often between the bandages, to protect the dead from negative influences and help them in their crossing. One of the most important was the heart scarab, which was placed directly over the heart of the dead. This amulet had the function of ensuring that the heart did not betray its owner during the weighing before Osiris. Other amulets, such as the ankh (symbol of life) and the djed (pillar of stability), were used to ensure the protection and resurrection of the soul, reaffirming its connection with the divine.

The moment of burial, in turn, was shrouded in solemnity and mystery. The carefully constructed tomb symbolized the underworld, where the body would rest, but the soul would continue its journey. Inside the tomb, in addition to the amulets and sacred texts, food, drinks, and everyday objects were placed, which would be used by the deceased in their new life. This attention to detail demonstrated the Egyptian belief in eternal life and the fact that, although the body remained on earth, the soul would continue its existence in the realm of the gods.

Funerals were moments of intense spiritual connection, where the role of priests and family was fundamental. Women, especially, played a prominent role, leading funeral laments and invoking protective goddesses, such as Nephthys and Isis, to protect the soul of the deceased. These laments, accompanied by symbolic gestures and prayers, were part of the farewell ritual, ensuring that the soul had a peaceful crossing and that the body was honored with due respect.

With the conclusion of the rituals, the soul of the deceased was finally prepared to continue its journey through the afterlife.

When the soul embarked on its journey through the Duat, the Egyptian underworld, it found itself facing a dark and labyrinthine reality, full of dangers and challenges. This spiritual realm, ruled by Osiris, was a vast landscape where gods, demons, and mystical creatures coexisted, representing a series of tests that the soul needed to overcome to achieve eternal life. The rituals that accompanied this passage were not just physical preparations, but spiritual guides that ensured that the spirit of the deceased had the tools necessary to traverse this realm of mystery and resurrection.

The crossing through the Duat was seen as a nocturnal journey, a path that followed the cycle of the sun. Just as the sun disappeared on the horizon and traveled through the darkness of the underworld to be reborn the next day, the soul also needed to go through the spiritual night before emerging in the realm of the gods. The dead, now enveloped in the rituals that prepared them, carried with them the enchantments and magic formulas of the "Pyramid Texts" or the "Book of the Dead," which were used as maps to guide the soul along the dangerous roads of the underworld.

Each stage of the journey was protected by deities and guarded by beings that could divert or destroy the soul if it was not properly prepared. At this point, the strength of the enchantments inscribed in the tombs and amulets began to manifest. One of the most important rituals for this crossing was the recitation of specific formulas designed to open gates, ward off demons, or even persuade deities to allow safe passage. The soul of the deceased, upon encountering these spiritual barriers, needed to identify itself with the correct name and words of power, and thus ensure that its path remained free of traps.

The role of amulets, such as the heart scarab and the ankh, became vital as the soul approached the most critical moments of the journey. The scarab, which protected the heart during judgment, ensured that the heart did not betray its bearer. The ankh, a symbol of eternal life, reminded the gods and guardians of the underworld that the soul was destined to be reborn. These sacred objects, imbued with power during funeral rituals, acted as shields against the negative energies that surrounded the Duat, ensuring that the deceased was always protected.

As the journey unfolded, the soul finally approached the most feared and awaited moment: the judgment before Osiris. The ritual of weighing the heart was the culmination of this crossing. Before an assembly of gods, including Thoth, who recorded the result, and Ma'at, who held the feather of truth and justice, the heart of the deceased was placed on a scale. This heart, with all the memories and actions of life, should be lighter than or equal to the feather of Ma'at, symbol of cosmic balance.

The rite of weighing was not just a moral judgment, but also a cosmic event. The lightness of the heart indicated that the soul had lived according to the principles of ma'at, universal harmony. However, if the heart proved heavy with the burdens of imbalance, selfishness, or injustice, the soul would be condemned. Ammit, the devourer of souls, a hybrid creature of crocodile, lion, and hippopotamus, waited patiently. If the heart was heavier, Ammit would devour the soul, preventing it from reaching eternal life and condemning it to eternal oblivion.

If the soul passed the weighing of the heart, it was welcomed by Osiris and the gods of the afterlife. At that moment, the deceased was transformed into a divine being, an "Akh," and received the privilege of living eternally in the fields of Aaru, a kind of Egyptian paradise. This field, described as a fertile land with rivers and eternal plantations, was the place where righteous souls could enjoy a new life, caring for their fields, surrounded by abundance, but without the burdens of physical existence. Funeral rituals, with their offerings of food and tools, ensured that the soul was prepared for this new life cycle, as everything that had been deposited in the tomb would be available in the afterlife.

To ensure that the soul continued to thrive in the afterlife, family members and priests performed periodic rituals after death, offering food, drinks, and prayers in the funerary chapels. The Egyptians believed that, even after judgment and arrival in paradise, the soul needed to be spiritually nourished. The funerary statues, which represented the deceased, served as receptacles for these offerings, allowing the soul, now deified, to continue to interact with the world of the living and receive the vital energy necessary to maintain its existence in the afterlife.

Funeral texts, such as the "Book of the Dead," further described the enchantments needed to protect the soul in its new life. The words of power, inscribed in the tombs and amulets, continued to act as constant protection. Although the body remained on earth, preserved and guarded by the force of rituals, the soul lived free, navigating the waters of the celestial Nile, where light and darkness coexisted in balance. The death ritual, therefore, was more than a closure — it was a transition, a continuous process of spiritual renewal, where the soul freed itself from physical limitations and merged with the eternal.

In the end, the fate of the soul was not simply determined by death itself, but by the degree of preparation and purity that the individual had cultivated in life. Rituals, therefore, were not mere funeral formalities, but a testament to the Egyptian belief in the interconnection between life, death, and rebirth. For those who successfully passed through these ritual and spiritual stages, eternity was a promise fulfilled, a new existence where the cycle of life and death merged into a celestial harmony, in accordance with the gods and cosmic forces that governed the fate of all things.

Chapter 24
Post-Mortem Protection Rituals

The silence that enveloped the desert at night was profound, broken only by the soft whisper of the wind. In the vastness of sand and darkness, there was an ancient knowledge that permeated the air: the mystery of life after death. For the Egyptians, death was not the end, but a passage, a crossing to a new state of existence. And this journey needed to be protected.

Post-mortem protection rituals were essential to ensure that the spirit found its safe path through the underworld, a realm full of dangers, trials, and spiritual challenges. Without adequate protection, it was believed that the soul could be lost or destroyed by the chaotic forces of the afterlife. The gods, powerful intermediaries, were the guides and protectors on this journey, but it was up to the living to ensure that the correct rites were performed to invoke this protection.

Soon after the last breath, the preparation of the body began. Embalming was not just a practice of physical preservation, but a spiritual ritual. The body, wrapped in sacred oils and linen wrappings, was carefully prepared to face eternity. Each step of the process had a magical function. The perfumed resins used in mummification, for example, had the power to ward off evil spirits that might try to corrupt the body and soul. The amulets, positioned between the layers of fabric, carried magical formulas that guaranteed continuous protection.

Among the most powerful amulets was the Heart Scarab, a small, precisely carved jewel. Representing the god Khepri, the scarab symbolized rebirth and transformation. During the journey through the underworld, this amulet was placed over the deceased's heart, to ensure that, at the moment of judgment, the heart would not betray its owner. The magic words engraved on the scarab asked that the heart not reveal secrets that could condemn the soul in the court of Osiris.

In addition to the amulets, the Pyramid Texts and the Coffin Texts were essential to guide the soul on its journey. These texts, full of enchantments and prayers, were inscribed on the walls of tombs or on papyri placed beside the body. They contained detailed instructions on how to face each of the challenges of the underworld, from crossing the Lake of Fire to confronting the guardians of the portals. Words had power, and through them, the spirit armed itself against invisible dangers.

In the darkness of the tomb, the soul began its journey, while the body, wrapped in silence, rested protected. For the living, the role of rituals did not end with burial. On the contrary, they continued through daily offerings and prayers. The families of the deceased regularly visited the tombs to deposit food, perfumes, and flowers. These offerings, it was believed, nourished the ka - the vital spirit of the deceased - ensuring that he had the strength to continue his journey.

The priests, in turn, played a fundamental role in this process. They recited incantations during funeral ceremonies and ensured that the deceased's name was repeated in prayers and offerings. In Ancient Egypt, to be forgotten was equivalent to true death, and the priests ensured that the names of those who had departed were perpetuated, bringing them a form of immortality.

Post-mortem protection rituals were also a way of ensuring that the spirit reached paradise. The Aaru, the reed fields, was the desired final destination, where the soul could live in peace and abundance, far from the torments of the underworld. To reach this paradise, the rituals had to be performed precisely, and the soul needed to prove itself worthy in the court of Osiris, where its heart would be weighed against the feather of truth, the feather of Ma'at.

In the silence of the tombs and the stillness of the desert, the rituals reverberated through time. Each amulet, each prayer, and each offering were steps on an invisible but powerful journey that transcended death. For the Egyptians, eternity was not guaranteed, but conquered through ritualistic protection that ensured that the soul completed its journey and found peace in the afterlife.

In the heart of the burial chambers, where eternal darkness enveloped the body of the deceased, the deepest secrets of the soul awaited their release. The tomb was more than a dwelling place for the dead; it was a portal to hidden dimensions, and the rituals that unfolded there ensured that the soul would not be lost in this labyrinth of shadow and light.

The inscriptions on the walls of the tombs revealed the spiritual map needed for this crossing. The Coffin Texts, written with meticulous precision, were a compendium of enchantments that protected the spirit on its journey. Each word, each symbol carved in stone, echoed with the force of an ancestral spell. These magic formulas were not simple prayers; they carried the power to shape invisible realities, to open paths between the world of the living and the realm of the dead. Among the most powerful enchantments was the "Chapter of Raising the Sky," a formula that allowed the deceased to pass through the portals that led to the stars.

The gods played an essential role in this journey. The deceased, often represented as Osiris in his renewed state, was guided by Anubis, the god of the dead, who watched over the purity of his soul and ensured that the correct rites were followed. In the Pyramid Texts, older and more mysterious, the enchantments evoked the elevation of the spirit to unite with the sky, not just as a soul, but as a star among the gods. The ultimate goal of the dead was to achieve eternity among the stars, becoming a constellation in the firmament, a divine and eternal being.

Within this vision, post-mortem protection was not just a matter of physical or spiritual preservation; it was about ensuring that the soul reached its cosmic destiny. The ka, the vital principle, needed to be nourished through constant offerings made by the living. These gifts, placed on altars near the grave, offered energy for the spirit to continue its journey without weakening. There was a complex network of exchanges between the worlds: the dead depended on the living to maintain their strength, and the living, in turn, believed that the spirits of their ancestors protected and guided them in times of difficulty.

The funerary figures, the ushabtis, small servants in the form of statues, were buried along with the deceased to fulfill their tasks in the afterlife. Carrying small tools in their hands, these figures ensured that the dead were not disturbed by mundane work in the underworld. Activated by specific enchantments, they carried out the orders that the deceased might receive from the gods in the afterlife, freeing him to focus on his own spiritual ascension.

Still, the passage through the underworld was full of trials. One of the most feared moments was the judgment of the soul before Osiris. In the sacred chamber, the heart of the dead was placed on a scale, on one side, and on the other, the feather of Ma'at, symbol of truth and cosmic order. This was the moment of greatest tension for the deceased. If the heart was heavier than the feather, the soul would be devoured by Ammit, a terrible creature with the body of a lion, hippopotamus, and crocodile. To avoid such a fate, the rituals and enchantments performed during life and at the time of death should ensure that the heart was pure.

The Book of the Dead was an essential guide for this judgment. Filled with instructions and enchantments, it contained what the Egyptians called the "Negative Confession" - a list of sins that the soul claimed not to have committed in life. By reciting this confession before the 42 judges of the afterlife, the dead ensured that their heart would not betray them on the scales. This text, inscribed on papyri and deposited in the tomb, accompanied the deceased as a spiritual weapon.

Post-mortem protection, therefore, extended beyond the physical body and entered the spheres of morality and truth. It was not enough to ensure that the body was preserved or that the enchantments were correctly recited. Life itself should be lived according to the principles of Ma'at, so that at the final moment, before Osiris, the soul could remain light and true, worthy of crossing the underworld and being reborn among the stars.

Thus, in the midst of the desert, the tombs stood as monuments not only to death, but to the journey beyond it. Each ritual, each offering, each enchantment was a link in the chain that connected the deceased to the cosmos. As the living laid their gifts before the tombs, the silence was broken only by the soft murmur of enchantments whispered by the priests, ensuring that the spirit, protected by their words and offerings, found its place in the eternal firmament.

Chapter 25
Rituals of Connection with the Cosmos and the Stars

In their silent nights, the ancient Egyptians would gaze upon the sky and see more than just stars. Each point of light that twinkled in the celestial dome was a living part of the cosmos, a manifestation of the divine forces that governed Earth and human destiny. To them, the sky was not distant; it was a reflection of what occurred in the world of the gods and, at the same time, a guide for their own steps.

The sacred temples, built with an almost supernatural precision, were aligned with astronomical events of great importance. At certain times of the year, when the stars reached specific positions, the doors of these temples would open for rituals that connected the earthly world to the firmament. These rituals were performed with deep respect, as it was believed that within them lay the secret to maintaining balance between cosmic cycles and life on Earth.

In the darkness of the desert, priests would gather on nights of eclipse, when the power of the stars and the sky became palpable. Absolute silence reigned as they drew on the sacred ground the symbols that mirrored distant constellations. Each figure drawn represented a star or a planet, and the gods that inhabited these spheres were invoked through ancestral chants.

At the temple of Karnak, one of the most important spiritual centers of Egypt, the alignment with the Winter Solstice was eagerly awaited. On this day, the rays of Ra would penetrate directly into the temple's interior, illuminating the sacred statue. This moment, prepared for weeks in advance, was a clear sign of the union between heaven and earth, and the divine power that descended to mortals.

But it was not only solar events that guided the Egyptians. They carefully observed the movement of stars and planets. The appearance of Sirius, the brightest star in the night sky, marked the beginning of the Nile floods, a crucial phenomenon for the fertility of the land. It was during this time that grand ceremonies were held, thanking the gods for another cycle of life, while the priests and the pharaoh himself participated in rituals to ensure the waters were abundant and beneficial.

The initiates, those who had undergone rituals of purification and wisdom, were led into the desert during certain nights, where they would lie beneath the vast starry sky. There, through deep meditation, they connected with the mysteries of the universe, feeling their souls float among the stars. It was said that in these moments, the gods spoke directly to those who were ready to listen, revealing secrets about destiny and the cosmic order.

The guidance of the stars also determined political and military decisions. Before a great battle, priests consulted the stars, seeking signs in the stars and planets to predict the unfolding of events. The sky was read as a sacred text, where the future was written. Each celestial movement had meaning, and the gods communicated with men through these signs.

On one such night, as the clear sky reflected the brilliance of the Milky Way, a priest of the temple of Horus felt something shift. The air seemed heavier, and the stars, closer than ever, seemed to pulsate in a slow, hypnotic dance. He knew that something important was about to happen - a change, a new cycle.

The deepest secrets of Egyptian astrology were not available to all. Only the highest priests, those who dedicated their lives to the study of the heavens, fully understood the forces that governed the firmament and, consequently, the Earth. They would gather in small groups, under the silence of the inner chambers of the temples, to interpret celestial movements with the help of ancient sacred texts, carefully written on papyri preserved for generations.

It was known that each star and each constellation had a story, and each was connected to a god or cosmic entity. The divinity that resided in Orion, for example, was closely associated with Osiris, the god of resurrection. For the Egyptians, the cycle of birth, death, and rebirth was mirrored in the stars, and Orion, with its intense brightness, symbolized the eternal power of Osiris, guiding the souls of the dead on their journey to the afterlife.

During planetary alignments, rare and important moments, priests performed complex rituals that could last entire nights. It was believed that these alignments opened portals between the mortal world and the divine realm. The power of the planets, as well as their position in the sky, directly influenced the fate of Egypt, and rituals were performed to ensure that this influence was beneficial. Incense of rare herbs was burned, their smoke rising as offerings to the gods, while ancient prayers echoed through the temples.

The pharaoh, as the representative of the gods on Earth, played a central role in these rituals. When the gods sent signs through the stars, it was to the pharaoh that they entrusted the final interpretation. At certain times, he himself would perform a solitary vigil, observing the sky in search of a vision or an omen that could change the course of his reign. Divine power would flow through him, strengthening his spirit and preparing him for the decisions that lay ahead.

The "Dendera Zodiac," a celestial map engraved in stone on the ceiling of an ancient temple, was one of the tools used by priests to interpret fate. Through this zodiac, they were able to understand the cosmic cycles that governed nature and human life, predicting important events such as births, deaths, and changes in power. Each star, each planet, had an influence on the destiny of men, and it was the duty of the priests to ensure that balance was maintained.

In the desert, far from the lights and noise of the city, the most intimate rituals of connection with the cosmos took place under the light of the moon and stars. It was in these moments of deep silence that the priests felt the pulse of the universe, their hearts beating in unison with the movement of the stars. It was believed that by aligning their souls with the cosmos, they could not only predict the future but also influence it.

The pyramids, majestic and mysterious, were more than just tombs. Their orientation in relation to the cardinal points and stars meant that they were also portals, connecting Earth to the sky, and the pharaohs buried within them were transported directly to the stars, where they would reside alongside the gods. Thus, the pyramids continued to play their role in cosmic balance, being monuments of eternal power, vibrating with the energy of the universe.

It was said that at certain times, the cosmos itself spoke. Slow movements of stars, meteor showers, or the unexpected appearance of a new star were considered direct signs from the gods, and each event was interpreted with utmost reverence. It was believed that these stars that appeared without warning were divine messengers, bearers of inevitable changes, and were treated with great respect.

In the final connection between Earth and the stars, Egypt found its harmony. Each ritual, each prayer, and each offering reinforced the link between the gods and men, between heaven and Earth, perpetuating the eternal cycle of ma'at, the cosmic order that guided the universe. The stars were not just distant lights; they were part of a living, pulsating network, and the Egyptians, with their ancestral knowledge, were able to walk among them, carrying with them the secrets of the cosmos.

Chapter 26
Rituals of Spiritual Ascension and Union with the Gods

A profound silence filled the temple's interior. Stars glittered in the firmament, but within, where only the echo of the pharaoh's footsteps could be heard, the connection with the divine became palpable. The pharaoh was no longer merely a man; he was about to unite with the gods, to ascend to the spiritual plane, in one of ancient Egypt's most sacred and hidden rituals.

The priests guided him slowly, leading him through corridors bathed in incense, where statues of deities observed him intently. It was as if each figure guarded the mysteries of the universe, secrets to ordinary mortals, but within reach of those prepared for transcendence. The pharaoh's journey began there, a path of purification and transformation that would connect him directly to the cosmos.

At the heart of the temple, a chamber of solid stone housed the most sacred symbols. There, the pharaoh knelt before a golden statue of Osiris, the god of resurrection and eternal life. This was the first step of ascension. Just as Osiris had risen, the pharaoh, alive in the flesh, was preparing for the symbolic death that would grant him the right to walk among the gods.

Around him, the priests chanted ancient hymns, voices echoing in unison with the energy of the universe. They knew each verse by heart, passed down through generations, carefully preserved on the walls of temples and tombs. Each sound, each word, held mystical power, a frequency that vibrated within the pharaoh's body, preparing him for his ascension.

Purification began with the sacred water of the Nile, symbolizing rebirth. The pharaoh was bathed with this water, cleansing not only his body but also his soul, readying him to transcend the physical world. After the ritual bath, amulets were placed upon his body, carefully positioned at vital points to protect his spirit during the spiritual journey.

The climax of the ritual involved invoking the principal gods, especially Ra, the sun god, whose light would guide the pharaoh through the higher spheres. A solitary flame was lit, representing the light of creation, and then the pharaoh was invited to walk towards the fire. In doing so, he became the bearer of this divine light, absorbing the power of Ra into his very essence.

At that moment, time seemed to dissolve. The pharaoh was between the physical and spiritual worlds, between life and death. He was no longer a mere man, but a being of light, an ascending spirit. The gods awaited him, ready to receive him among them.

Night deepened as the pharaoh, now deeply immersed in spiritual ecstasy, advanced towards the unknown. The temple walls no longer seemed like simple stone, but vibrant portals, leading his soul to dimensions beyond mortal comprehension. Around him, the air pulsed with invisible energy, as if the cosmos itself was watching, waiting to welcome him.

The priests, in silent devotion, stepped back, creating a protective circle around the altar. They knew that, in that instant, the pharaoh no longer belonged to the earth. He was a bridge between worlds, a being who, through ancient rituals, was shedding his last earthly bonds to unite with the gods. The magical words they had chanted still lingered in the air, like echoes guiding the pharaoh's spirit along the luminous path.

Before him, at the center of the altar, the sacred flame of Ra flickered, connecting heaven and earth. This fire, fueled by rare oils and herbs, should never be extinguished. It represented eternal life and the divine energy that propelled the cycle of the universe. The pharaoh approached, eyes fixed on the fire, feeling its warmth penetrate deep into his skin and soul. The golden light was a reflection of the supreme union he was about to achieve, a communion as ancient as time itself.

There, before the flame, he prepared for the final phase of ascension. His meditation was profound, his mind detached from worldly distractions. In his inner vision, he saw the gods gathered in a great hall of light. Anubis, with his solemn presence, stood at the door, waiting to guide him beyond the veils of mystery. Isis and Osiris watched from afar, recognizing in him the power of a divine heir.

The pharaoh, in his trance, recited incantations learned in his sacred training. Each word was a step forward in the spiritual plane, elevating his consciousness to new levels. He felt his physical body receding, his soul expanding beyond the limits that had contained it for so long. The constellations, the same that had guided his kingdom and his decisions, were now part of his essence.

The culmination of the ritual involved the full embodiment of a god. It was the moment when the pharaoh not only worshipped but temporarily became the deity he had always served. Overwhelming energy flowed through him, and the room seemed to vibrate with his presence. The pharaoh was, in that moment, an extension of Ra, a channel through which cosmic power flowed freely. He felt every beat of the universe within him, every pulse of the stars in the far reaches of the cosmos.

Then, at the peak of his union with the divine, the pharaoh knew he had crossed the threshold. There was no longer any separation between him and the gods. His flesh and spirit were in complete synchrony with the primordial forces, and for a brief moment, he touched eternity. When he returned to his mortal form, he would do so transformed, endowed with an invisible yet undeniable power.

The priests watched in reverence, understanding the significance of that moment. They knew that the pharaoh's return would be silent, his voice perhaps deeper, his gaze more distant, for he had seen and felt what few mortals could ever comprehend.

Epilogue

Throughout this work, we have journeyed along the mystical paths that the ancient Egyptians masterfully trod, unveiling secrets that date back to an era when the divine and the human were intimately intertwined. Through detailed rituals and wisdom passed down through generations, Egypt has taught us to live in harmony with cosmic forces, to understand the crucial role of magic in maintaining universal balance, and to see the world as a reflection of the invisible energies that shape it.

We conclude this journey with the certainty that the knowledge explored here goes beyond what is visible to the eye. Each ritualistic gesture, each chanted word, each amulet charged with power not only manifests protection or healing but reveals the profound link between humanity and the cosmos. The Egyptians knew that magic was the thread connecting the everyday to the eternal, and this same connection can still be re-established by those who dare to access the invisible, who allow themselves to open the doors of mystery.

At the heart of this wisdom lies Ma'at, the cosmic order that must be maintained in all aspects of life. Reflecting on all that we have learned, it becomes clear that Ma'at was not merely a philosophical or religious concept but a living reality that permeated every action of the Egyptians. From the simplest rituals performed within homes to the grand ceremonies in temples, every gesture aimed to restore or maintain balance. This notion applies directly to our lives today. If we pause to consider, we will see that the challenges, imbalances, and difficulties we face are largely reflections of a disconnection from this primordial order.

The knowledge imparted by this work invites us to restore this harmony. Through the rituals described, we can reconnect with the forces that govern the universe. It is not simply a matter of reproducing ancient practices but of understanding their deeper meanings and applying them to our time. The power of magic, as the Egyptians conceived it, resides in the intention and awareness that everything in the universe is interconnected.

Just as they looked to the stars for guidance, we too must remember that the cosmos is full of signs, waiting to be deciphered. The Egyptians knew that the stars were not merely points of light in the sky but living entities, spiritual guides. The alignment of temples with astronomical events was not a coincidence but an expression of their profound respect and understanding of cosmic forces. This connection between Earth and sky, between the physical and the spiritual, reminds us that there is much more beyond what our immediate senses can grasp.

Now, as we close this book, the invitation it extends to us is clear: we must continue exploring this knowledge, applying it to our lives, and keeping alive the flame of mystery that the ancient Egyptians bequeathed to us. Learning does not end here. On the contrary, it opens the doors to a new phase of discovery. What has been revealed must now be internalized and put into practice, for only then can we truly understand the scope of these ancestral truths.

May this be just the beginning of your journey. The magic that once permeated Egypt is still present, awaiting those who, with open hearts and minds, wish to re-establish contact with the eternal. May you go forth, carrying with you the teachings and energies that shaped the most enigmatic civilization in history. The path is laid out. Now, it is up to you to follow.

www.ingramcontent.com/pod-product-compliance
Lightning Source LLC
LaVergne TN
LVHW041939070526
838199LV00051BA/2843